*To Joanne,
Very best
wishes.
Shirley
Ilkley 12/10/09*

Region / Writing / Home
RELOCATING DIASPORIC WRITING IN BRITAIN

VOLUME 9 NUMBER 2 2009

Moving Worlds is a biannual international magazine. It publishes creative, critical, literary, and visual texts. Contributions of unpublished material are invited. Books for notice are welcome. Manuscripts should be double-spaced with footnotes gathered at the end, and should conform to the MHRA (Modern Humanities Research Association) Style Sheet. Wherever possible the submission should be on disc (soft-ware preferably Word for Windows, Wordperfect or Macwrite saved for PC on PC formatted disc) and should be accompanied by a hard copy. Please include a short biography, address, and email contact if available.

   Moving Worlds is an internationally refereed journal based at the University of Leeds. The editors do not necessarily endorse the views expressed by its contributors.

All correspondence – manuscripts, books for review, enquiries – should be sent to: The Editor, *Moving Worlds*, School of English, University of Leeds, Leeds LS2 9JT, UK

email: mworlds@leeds.ac.uk
http://www.movingworlds.net

SUBSCRIPTION RATES FOR 2009
Individuals: 1 year £25.00
Institutions: 1 year £50.00
Students: 1 year £10.00
Cheques should be made payable to: University of Leeds (Moving Worlds)
Payment is accepted by Visa or Mastercard, please contact Moving Worlds for details

Published by
Moving Worlds, at School of English
University of Leeds
Leeds
LS2 9JT UK

ISBN 978-0-9553060-6-8   ISSN 1474-4600

Contents

Acknowledgements

Moving Worlds is published with funding assistance from the School of English, University of Leeds.

We would like to thank all the contributors to this journal

Artwork in 'Changing Identities, Changing Spaces' pp. 80-95
by kind permission of the artist Zahir Rafiq; exhibition photography Steve Wright

Cover illustrations:
Front: Michael Gutteridge, 'Tram Between St. Peter's Square and G-Mex', 2005
40x50cm, acrylic on board
By kind permission of the artist
Back: Zahir Rafiq, 'Hope Street', 2005, detail, medium digital
By kind permission of the artist

Editorial

CORINNE FOWLER & GRAHAM MORT

> But the particular mix of social relations which are thus part of what defines the uniqueness of any place is by no means all included in that place itself. Importantly, it includes relations which stretch beyond – the global as part of the local, the outside as part of the inside. Such a view of place challenges any possibility of claims to internal histories or to timeless identities. And the particularity of any place is, in these terms, constructed not by placing boundaries around it and defining its identity through counter-position to the other which lies beyond, but precisely (in part) through the specificity of the mix of links and interconnections to that 'beyond'. The identities of place are always, unfixed, contested and multiple. Places viewed this way are open and porous.   Doreen Massey, *Space, Place, and Gender*

It is only very recently that postcolonial and diaspora scholars have embarked on the systematic study of localized inflections. Academic work on the interface between the global and the regional has necessarily involved recuperating and cataloguing the artistic and literary outputs of particular cities or regions. This issue of *Moving Worlds* attends to the range and scope of writing that such projects are bringing to the discussion. Grounded in the thousand places, and the sixty million individuals and their relationships that make up Britain, the sheer diversity of this writing confounds any attempt either to homogenize 'Britain' by defining it in national terms or to present London as the literary hub of diaspora. Insofar as the regional/metropolitan division in Britain can be seen as a microcosm of divisive colonial binaries, this last concern is connected to long running debates about the designation of writing as 'regional', together with some consideration of its consequences for access to publishers and national readerships.

Region/Writing/Home puts four major research projects into dialogue: 'Beyond the Book: Mass Reading Events and Contemporary Cultures of Reading', 'Artefacts and narratives of migration: Rotherham museum collections and the Pakistani/ Kashmiri community of Rotherham', 'Devolving Diasporas: Migration and Reception in Central Scotland, 1980 – present', and 'Moving Manchester/Mediating Marginalities'. Building on the legacy of these projects are additional essays by researchers whose work on diaspora is focused on the interface between the global and the regional.

The editors have commissioned a contrapuntal body of new creative work for which the relationship between the global and the local provides a specific remit. The writers concerned occupy a regional location while demonstrating a strong awareness of the contradictions and possibilities of simultaneous belongings. The result is work that draws attention to the way that human consciousness both assimilates and generates experience: what does a 'sense of place' signify when places themselves are simultaneously actual and virtual, both experienced by and projected from the coordinating centres of human consciousness? In this analysis, 'sense' quickly takes precedence over 'place', showing human location and its cultural expression to be contingent upon individual and collective consciousness, and the reflexive cycles of individual and collective experience.

Ian Duhig, Fadia Faqir, Basir Kasmi, Muli Amaye, John Siddique, Dinesh Allirajah and Moniza Alvi have contributed both prose and poetry that explore the commonplace of *de facto* belonging or of being *in transit*. Their writing expresses an awareness and synthesis of locations that is decentred in the metropolitan sense: even when London is the setting, it is not conceptualized as a unitary entity so much as a series of locales. Inflections of regionality are also levelled, from the more belligerent stance of an earlier generation of 'northern' writers to a more subtle sense of location as being, not necessarily confining, so much as where we happen to begin. Intriguingly, literature itself – the prose story and the poem – emerges as locations inhabited by writers and readers not only in the sense that writing expresses a 'sense of place', but because it is where consciousness gets 'lost', energized and enlarged.

Grouped according to their regional affiliations, or disaffiliations, the essays and creative pieces included in *Region/Writing/Home* are set in Liverpool, Leeds, London, Manchester, Rotherham and Sheffield. These urban locations are viewed through the conceptual and aesthetic lenses of 'elsewheres' that incorporate the Caribbean, India, Pakistan, Ireland, Eastern Europe, the Middle-East, Africa and Sri Lanka, among others. Their variety and range defy definition, creating a fitting counterpart to the intersecting complexities of their subject matter.

The 'Moving Manchester' project itself revealed how complex the definition of place can be as its preliminary audit surveyed the world's first great manufacturing city. That commercial definition (a metaphor for literary production, perhaps) leads us into the complexity of a hinterland that absorbed imports of raw material from the British empire and supplied the Port of Manchester with finished goods. Greater Manchester exceeds its official postcode, drawing in the satellite towns of Rochdale, Burnley, Bolton, Blackburn, Oldham and Ashton-under-Lyne as well as Alexandria, Cairo, Bombay, Calcutta, Dublin, Lagos and other globally interconnected cities.

The archaeology of urban spaces is central to the heritage industry, which relies on a city's buildings, rather than its inhabitants, to reconstruct versions of the past. Yet what defines a city on the map – the arterial network of roads and the solid blocks of built-up areas and significant centres – means little without the inhabitants and their movement within and beyond the city. In this sense, maps themselves may be re-drawn as paradigms of consciousness. Not hard-wired like old 'computational' maps of the human brain, but multi-dimensional, constantly evolving, infinitely complex, subtly responsive and constituted of a nexus of pathways and journeys. This model, where beyond is constitutive of within, where the experience of place triggers memory, experience, and anticipation of elsewhere, has to be seen as existing outside, within, and *because of* human consciousness.

Debates about the regional inflections of diaspora are taking place within increasingly mobile definitions of place, space, and community; just as writers in many former colonies would prefer to be ex- rather than post-colonial, writers in regional Britain increasingly refuse their location as historically binding. The result is diversity in scholarly discussion and literary output that unpicks the old taxonomies of belonging into something far more contingent and devolved.

JOHN SIDDIQUE

A Seed to a Flower, the Simplest Thing

THE MOVING MANCHESTER COMMISSION
FIVE POEMS FROM REAL LIVES

Jali

Returning from the sun to return to his son.
Bouncing harp notes from the plate glass
of Superdrug.

Cutting the air with proud chin,
with cigarette smoke, with music passed
from his father's hands into his fingers.
Returning from Gambia to return to his son.

The kora is life. Life in Piccadilly Gardens
made clean and crystal, lifted spirit,
as we approach and leave.
Intersections of buses and trams;
Altrincham one way, Bury the other.
Crosscutting the notes of time and pitch
to hold his life together.

Humanity is different here, he says.
People don't know about each other.
Music penetrates us with imported humanity.
I don't play for money, I play for our souls.

There are bargains to be had in Superdrug,
two deodorants for the price of one.
Away down Market Street there are other musics,
the loop of a Romanian waltz played on accordion,
a French tango by the escalators near the shoe shops.

If you come here before the music starts,
you have to imagine the life of the city.
Jali with his kora, his amp and car battery
for power, riding in on the silver tram
as the shoppers gather. Chiming in the cold sun,
in the landscaped square where we pass by,
leaving our trails as music on the air.

Kitying

Becomes Crystal
       – changing state at the age of twelve.

Makes a new name with her left hand,
cutting the facets of each letter with intention.

Polishing smooth each cut to gleam in the light.
Puts her foot forward
       – changing state, when standing still.

She has made herself, made herself, made herself
become Crystal
       – Kitying from Hong Kong.

Helps her mother with the left hand of duty and love.
Gets lost watching Eastenders, letting go of all the making.

Stands in two worlds with two names.
Pausing for breath when the money runs out.

Changing state:
Looking at the sky as the starlings flock and swoop.
To be only flight, the transparency of movement.

Changing state:
Compressing feathers to carbon, carbon to Crystal.

Clear as the light first thing in the morning.
Still and always in flight, she is making herself.

Abha

The Earth loves the first ray of light that falls
upon him each morning more than any other light.

She is the first ray, the only one.
Day has its beauty but nothing pleases the Earth
more than the first moment when Abha takes his hand.

What a risk to take for love?
Five thousand miles and a failing marriage,
a cat's cradle of ties holding her there.

Moving with the sunlight as it tracks his face
he is the world under her; without each other
there is only darkness and bare rock.

What did the Earth know before
the first ray of light of the morning?
That darkness was all and forever.
His hardness, the absence of life.
A cold dream of a star.
The meaning of being untouched.

What did the light know before
she reached out to take Earth's hand?
Pure speed through endless darkness.
No reflection of herself in the mirror.
A cold dream of a distant Earth.
The meaning of not touching.

From Chandigarh to Manchester
for a man she only knows by heart
        – the imagined city of love.
Imagine a city without light,
or the light without a city.
How small the world of the heart?

The world has conurbated,
it's a small world they say.

How large the world is
when travelled for love,
when we count the hours
and the miles lived without it.

Maria

One. Two. Three.
When she got up that morning, she looked in
on the children still in their beds. She went
downstairs and made sweet tea.

Holding hands in a line as they walk,
no looking back at the family house
they can't afford any more.

A wren on a gatepost pays them no heed.
Her eyes fill with tears. The wren flies away.

A train across Europe, counting long hours.
Trees zip past. A ferry. Another train.
An address on a piece of paper.
Not imagining the city or the next day.
She hums a waltz to the children,
one, two, three.

Two. Two. Three.
Black scarf to keep her warm,
accordion on her chest.
An empty waltz for shoppers,
you can almost sing along.

Back before she left him
they would have danced to this
on Friday nights, counting time
in Bucharest, in the dim lights
of the dance hall, a round of drinks
waiting at their table.

Endless night of footsteps
counting the time of their marriage,
two, two, three.

Three. Two. Three.
Harp music from up towards Piccadilly.
The blast of sound from HMV.
Always the same position against the pillar,
British Home Stores. This is the waltz
of a woman who has made herself invisible
by the lowering of her eyes.

Her children teach her English
though she never likes to speak it.
The same few notes every day.
The same faces of the shoppers every day.
The same looks. The same empty waltz.

There is a woman on market street who
is not there. She is waiting without waiting,
counting out time, three, two, three.

Junmo

Hibiscus petals falling – South Korea
puts her son on a plane for East Sussex,
you are the generations of family moving forward,
a strong brown river. Junmo's mouth is numb.

All around the boy is the rabble
of boarding school noise, they are the young
of wealthy aspiration, inheritors of the earth.

He is three months silent.
His numbness is extreme and perfect.
As they try to speak to him the pine tree
on the mountain stands unchanged.

At night he is a soldier, by the light
of his computer screen.
Lieutenant Jimmy Patterson moving
behind enemy lines. Thumbs moving
his mind through intrigue and heroics.

Language melts as wind and frost are blown away,
Roses of Sharon bloom as he moves
to northern quarters. Arms folded to keep his heart in.
A piecemeal plan:
sell hats,
make money,
buy a three-bedroom house.

Around him is the random noise of shoppers,
students, goths and new emos with their mums.
How will he inherit the earth?

In the end it's his breeding,
a simple act of belief passed on,
a seed to a flower, the simplest thing.

He would like someone to speak to him,
though he can't quite meet someone's eyes.
Saturday is the busiest day,
selling hats and leather-bound journals.
At night he is a soldier, his thumbs on the controller.

Note: this poem draws its shape and imagery from Ezra Pound's 'The Garden,' and The
South Korean National Anthem.

Accounting for the Life of Paul Cuffe

JOHN WHALE

> At 1PM Saw a Pilate Boat toward the Shore how [who] fired her Pilate Signall gunn
> We hawled our Wind for her + She keep for us At 2 P M We reicvd A Pilate who
> Directed our course S E by E for Liver Pool at 10 p m hove too [...] Arrived Safe all
> Well after a passage of 62 Days.[1]

On 12 July 1811, Paul Cuffe of Westport Massachusetts sailed up the Mersey into the port of Liverpool.[2] He was 65 days out from Sierra Leone in his own favourite vessel, a brig named *Traveller*. The voyage was an integral part of his last great project: the establishment of a commercially viable colony as the first stage in his larger historical vision for the 'improvement' and 'civilization' of what he conceived of as the national homeland of Africa.[3] The trip to England entailed financial deals with fellow Quaker merchants in Liverpool, including William and Richard Rathbone, William Allen, and Thomas Thompson, negotiations with the African Society in London, and the purchase of cargo from the new textile manufactories of Manchester. At a distance of only four years from Abolition and in the town which had been Britain's leading port in the iniquitous African trade since the 1760s,[4] the arrival of *Traveller* with her Black owner and crew had a major impact on the minds of the inhabitants. The *Edinburgh Review* was quick to recognize the irony:

> On the first of the present month of August 1811, a vessel arrived in Liverpool with a cargo from Sierra Leone, the owner, master, mate, and whole crew of which, were free Negroes. The master, who is also owner, is the son of an American slave, and is said to be very well skilled both in trade and navigation, as well as to be of a very pious and moral character. It must have been a strange and animating spectacle to see this free and enlightened African entering, as an independent trader, with his black crew, into that port which was so lately the *nidus* of the Slave Trade.[5]

In this essay I want to take up this 'strange and animating spectacle' and use the vantage-point provided by Paul Cuffe's iconic presence in Liverpool, what we might think of as a symbolic 'return' to the point of departure of the Atlantic triangle impacting on the guilty imagination of a nation, as a way of examining the meaning of his life. His story was construed in a variety of different texts: newspaper accounts, biographical sketches, a memorial discourse, and his own self-presentation in a series of log-books, journals, and letters. To account for the 'life' of Paul Cuffe, as we shall see, can take different forms, but all of them involve the simultaneous recognition and occlusion of different ethnicities. In a number of ways, then, the visual psychic shock of Cuffe's arrival in Liverpool might be seen as symptomatic and indicative of the larger story of his life; and the response it generated in print is immediately indicative of this story's conflicted mixture of self-determination and self-abnegation. To compound the irony noted by the *Edinburgh Review*, the entry into Liverpool also produced the first separately published account of Cuffe's life, which appeared initially in two instalments in the local newspaper, the *Mercury*, and, later, in pamphlet form, entitled *Memoir of Captain Paul Cuffe, a man of colour* (1811).[6]

Cuffe's biographers and editors have variously defined him: as an iconic hero of African-American achievement; a self-made 'man of colour' succeeding in maritime commerce against all the odds; as a pioneer challenger of state legislation and civil rights; and as a complex father of Black nationalism problematically implicated in setting a precedent for an 'African return'.[7] More recently, in a brief narrative coda to *Rough Crossings*, Simon Schama confirms this complex and, as I hope to suggest, anxious mixture when he describes Cuffe as 'an American patriot' and as 'a free black, landowner, trader, Quaker, and abolitionist'.[8] 'Black nationalist' and 'American patriot' are epithets which in themselves offer a source of potential conflict, but Cuffe's American identity is pushed, one might argue, to its limit by his identification with what he himself refers to as his 'African race'.[9] His scheme for 'repatriating' freed slaves in the West African colony of Sierra Leone, as we shall see, is premised on internationalist principles which challenge his more immediate geographical and cultural ties with his native New England. My focus here is the conflicted combination of economics and race to be found in the writing of Paul Cuffe's life which took place during his lifetime and in its immediate aftermath. These contemporaneous biographical accounts are themselves curious about the spectacle of a commercially successful black man inhabiting the new reality of post-Abolition Britain; for some, he appears as a providential manifestation of their cause; to others, he merely serves to point up the irony of historical difference, the novelty of the new era in which they find themselves. For Paul Cuffe himself, commercial enterprise is conceived of as the very means through which the ethical improvement of 'abolition' in a wider, world context can be brought about. For many of his supporters who shared his gradualist beliefs, it is his most powerful political legacy.

II

Many accounts of Paul Cuffe's arrival in Liverpool replicate the response in the *Edinburgh Review*. In their slight but significant differences, however, they reveal an anxiety in their representation of race, as if the new order of things in the post-Abolition era − in Britain at least − makes them peculiarly sensitive to the identification of race as skin colour. They exhibit a precarious and unstable mixture of popular curiosity and self-conscious ethical concern.

The following version from the *Liverpool Mercury* seems to have been syndicated; very similar versions appeared in *The Times* and the *Morning Chronicle*:

> The brig Traveller is just arrived from Sierra Leone, and is owned and commanded by Paul Cuffee, the son of 'Cuffee', a Negro slave imported into America. Her mate, and all her crew are Negroes, or the immediate descendents of Negroes − Captain Cuffee is about 50 years of age; has a wife (a Negress), and six children, living at New Bedford, Massachusetts, of which state he is a citizen …
>
> Capt. Cuffee is of a very pleasing countenance, and his physiognomy truly interesting; he is both tall and stout, speaks English well, dresses in the Quaker style, in a drab-coloured suit, and wears a large flapped white hat.[10]

The 'singular phenomenon' − as the *Morning Chronicle* described it − of Cuffe's appearance in the port of Liverpool speaks of a shock given to the visual imagination of the British public. The confident insistence on race is not matched by accuracy; Cuffe's wife, Alice Pequit, was not 'a Negress' as the newspaper puts it, but a Native American of the Pequot tribe. Captured in these two paragraphs is the challenging spectacle, for British readers at least, of Cuffe's blackness, but blackness combined with the surprising reassurance of disciplined sobriety, industry, and perseverance under the guise of Christian piety: what the *Mercury*, in response to Cuffe's mission to Sierra Leone describes as 'the blessings of British Christian benevolence'.[11] 'Respectability' here acts as the reverse to the visibility of race as skin colour and is an insistent part of the accounts. The narrative of Cuffe's life is prefaced, depending on the edition, with one of two quotations from William Cowper's poem, 'The Negro's Lament': 'Skins may differ, but affections/ Dwell in Blacks and Whites the same'; or 'Deem our nation brutes no longer,/ Till some reason ye shall find/ Worthier of regard, and stronger/ Than the colour of our kind'.[12] The 'nation' of the latter refers, of course, in the 1788 poem to the African nation, but here it resonates oddly in this − to the British conscience at least − most sensitive of post-Abolition contexts. The York edition of the *Memoir*, in more self-consciously liberal vein conjures this 'animating … spectacle for the eye of humanity' of a 'vessel trading to the port of Liverpool, commanded by a free and enlightened African' and 'not laden with instruments of cruelty and oppression, but manned with sable, yet free and respectable seamen, rescued from the galling chain of slavery, and employed in honourable commerce'.[13] The eye-witness account of the famous French-American Quaker preacher, Stephen Grellet, also focuses on the visibility of race: 'Paul Cuffe, a black man, owner and master of a vessel has come into port', he informs his reader, adding that 'the whole of his crew are black also'. After noting the 'general excitement' in the town, he suggests that, instead of guilty irony, the effect on the populace has been one of ethical education: 'it has, I believe, opened the minds of many in tender feelings towards the poor suffering Africans, who, they see, are men like themselves, capable of becoming, like Paul Cuffe, valuable and useful members of civil and religious society'.[14] In all these accounts, it is as if the conspicuous Black identity of *Traveller*'s crew must be in some way compensated for by their exemplary behaviour. Such ascriptions of respectable commerce, as we shall see, are the watchwords of Cuffe's self-representation and form the basis of his own ethics and politics of improvement.

III

Paul Cuffe's representation of himself is dominated by a self-abnegating piety compounded by a natural humility about his level of literacy. Modest disqualifiers about his lack of formal education – 'Please excuse my poor writing and bad spelling as I never had an opportunity of an hour school Learning'[15] – combine, in his later writings, with a firm conviction that the self be subjected to the workings of providence, that good works are what matter in the ultimate account of one's life.

The manner in which he signs off in a letter to William Allen is indicative: 'Lest I should wary thee I Shall Stop saying,/ I am Paul Cuffe'.[16] Not simply the expunging of ego in the face of others, but the assumption of his repeatedly, as it were, 'saying he is Paul Cuffe' captures the sense in which much of his writing assumes the status of a testament stretched across religious and financial boundaries. Writing itself assumes the status of a fiduciary act to which Paul Cuffe is automatically signatory. Identity, as one might expect here, is subjectivity determined by submission to God:

> As to Poor me I feel Very febel and all most Wornout in hard Service and uncapabel of doing much for my Brethren the afferican Race but blessed be god I am what I am and all that I Can Concive that god plese to Lay upon me to make an Insterment of me for that Service. I Desire Ever to be Submissive that his Will may be done &c.[17]

Within this 'service', the enigmatic 'I am what I am' of Paul Cuffe defines itself repeatedly as an instrument reacting to the dominating power of providence. Motivation, choice, and would-be acts of self-autonomy are repeatedly defined as forces or impressions acting upon and taking hold of his 'mind': 'it impressed on my mind'; 'I feel my mind Drawn towards thee'; 'my mind has been occupied'.[18] One of the most important 'events' to impress itself on Cuffe's mind in this way was his reading of Thomas Clarkson's *History of the Rise, Progress and Accomplishment of the Abolition of the African Slave-Trade* (1808) which he describes in his log in the following way:

> My time implyd in prusing Clarksons Records on abolishing Slavery which often Batized my mind in the Line of his proceeding &c my mind often times when Reumerreting With my friend at home Would Land Very over my head but in giveing my mind and Dependence on the allwise protector it Would afford me Consolation and Comfort[19]

Cuffe's awakening conviction is here described as a process of repeated baptisms which involves only tentative claims to understanding; it is no great, single revelation of truth. A gradualist perseverance affording consolation forms the heart of his thinking.

The practical unfolding of Cuffe's 'consolation' takes the form of a cannily strategic combination of commerce and morality. The process is, as he puts it in a letter to William Harris of Boston, one of 'Us[ing] all Good Aconomy to Improve our morals both in State and Society'.[20] Even in his African project he operates on this strategic basis; the population must 'be morralized before they are Christianized'.[21] His 'Remarks' for the fifth of the second month for 1812 reveal in an uncharacteristically metaphorical mode the degree to which his piety needs to take the form of steely, self-controlled prudence: 'when men are Like Lions We must be Carefull how We git our hands in their mouths and if We Should Chance to We must Endeavour to git out the Best Way of prudence. I hope this may be a Lessen of Instruction to me and not be unusefull to others'.[22] Cuffe's log is clearly conceived by its author as part of his exemplary life; and it is exemplary not just in its Quaker piety, but in its strategic awareness of how the cause of improvement and emancipation may, according to him, be best served by commercial advancement in conjunction with morality. Even his abolitionist sympathies and pan-Africanist projects seem to be motivated by the idea of the primacy of exemplary conduct as if that itself constituted a form of empowering righteousness: 'My mind has often been occupied for those who are held in a state of slavery and it has felt to me that the greatest aid we can render for their relief is that of faithfulness, honesty and uprightness in our selves'.[23] The cautionary side of his ethical response is evident in another entry: 'I note this in my minutes that the Peopel of Colour may See and Consider What Consolation We may See and Feel for Well Doing. But when We Commit Evel there is Grieff and Confusion attend us in Stead of Comfort.'[24]

Perhaps the most revealing instance of Cuffe's strategy of improvement through non-disruptive, exemplary conduct – his early nineteenth-century version of passive resistance in the manner of Rosa Parks in Montgomery Alabama in 1955 – is his uncharacteristically narrative account of racial prejudice on a stagecoach in Baltimore in 1812:

> When the Passangers Came in Came a busseling powder headed man With Starn Countenance 'Come *away* from the Seat.' I was no Starter and Set Still. He then Bustled along and Said 'I Wants to put my umbrell in the Box.' I arose he put his unbrela in. He then Saith 'You must go out of this for there is a Lady Comeing in'. I Entered into no Discourse With him but took my Seat. He took his beside me but Shew much Evel Contempt. At Length the Women and Girl made their appearance. I then arose and invited the Women in the after Seat Saying, 'We always gave away to accomadate the Women.' We Set forward on our journey. On our Way at the tavern I Was overtaken by Wm Hunter member of Congress. He was Very free and Conversant Which this man above mentioned observed. Before We got to Baltimore he became Loveing and openly accosted me, 'Captain take the after Seat.' But from Comon Custom I thanked him and Wished him to keep his Seat.
>
> I believe if I am favoured to keep my place my Enemies Will Become friendly. I note this for Encouragement of memory.[25]

Cuffe's pious and self-disciplined philanthropy is typically clinched here with his polite adherence to 'Comon Custom', optimistic in the knowledge that, through providence, he is 'favoured' and a conversion is possible in which 'Evel Contempt' turns to 'Loveing' and enemies can become friends.

IV

My last two texts offer startlingly contrasting accounts of the life of Paul Cuffe: one of them confidently establishes an African-American inheritance firmly located within the ethos of his path to social advancement, financial independence, Christian 'civilization' and engagement with Africa itself; the other exposes the buried native American inheritance present in most accounts of his life, including his own.

In the preface to *A Discourse Delivered on the Death of Paul Cuffee* in the African Methodist Zion Church New York in 1817, our subject is tellingly described as 'an American and a man of colour'; and in the main body of this apparently extempore oration the emphasis is firmly focused on his African identity, as we might expect of a text whose imagined audience is 'brethren of the African race in general' and whose opening rhetoric includes a reference to Cuffe's grave over which we're told: 'Europe and Africa mourn; and Africa, unhappy bereaved Africa, pours a deluge of tears'. While recognizing the non-partisan nature of his assistance to fellow human beings, Peter Williams, the African–American author of the discourse, asserts that it was 'in his active commiseration in behalf of his African brethren that [Cuffe] shone forth most conspicuously as a man of worth'. He asks his audience to consider him in 'his own phraseology, as a member of the whole African family'. 'Such was the warmth of his benevolence, the activity of his zeal, and the extent of his labours, in behalf of the African race', Williams suggests, 'his whole life may be said to have been spent in their service.' If the discourse confidently and exclusively appropriates Cuffe to the African-American cause in this way, it does so in a manner consistent with the image of him we have already witnessed: as a pious exemplum of unabrasive respectability. Once again, he is celebrated for his 'perseverance, prudence, and laudable enterprise'; and the challenge to the gathered audience is to proceed on this non-aggressive civilizing basis as the means to social inclusion and advancement. In 'a spirit of union and friendship', children, he urges, are to be 'instructed in the knowledge of letters, the necessary mechanical arts, and all the branches of useful science' as the community commits itself to 'endeavouring to rise to wealth, to knowledge and respectability'.[26]

If the discourse on his death accounts for the life of Paul Cuffe by insistent reference to his African ancestry, my last text, an account of the life of his son, Paul Cuffe Jr., proudly announces in its title another ethnicity with a very different inheritance and a very different sense of historical self-consciousness: *Narrative of the Life and Adventures of Paul Cuffe, A Pequot Indian, During Thirty Years Spent at Sea, and in Travelling in Foreign Lands* (1839). This 'Paul Cuffe' is immediately defined as 'a descendent of an Indian family, which formerly resided in the eastern part of Connecticut and constituted a part of that fierce and warlike tribe of Indians called Pequots, of whose exploits in the early Wars of New-England, the reader may become acquainted by perusing Trumbull's History of the Indian War'.[27] Prior to his conversion in 1808, Paul Cuffe senior had defined himself by turns as African and Native American. As part of a popular agitation to obtain civil rights in Massachusetts in 1780, he and

PAUL

CAPTAIN

CUFFEE

1812.

From a Drawing by JOHN POLE, M. D. of Bristol, Eng.

his brother, John, had petitioned the government as 'Indian men and by law not the subjects of taxation'. Like his father Kofi or Coffe Slocum – a freed slave, who had married Ruth Moses, a Gayhead Indian of the Wampanoag tribe in 1746 – Cuffe himself married Alice Pequit in 1783.[28] Accounting for the life of Paul Cuffe necessarily involves, it seems, an extraordinary process of exclusion and occlusion, especially if one's focus is on identity as single origin. In the case we have been following, self-determination and autonomy take the form of a Quaker conversion, and a commitment to a Black nationalism which is in danger of erasing key aspects of Cuffe's American ethnic, civic, and national identity. Lamont D. Thomas reads his 1812 image [opposite] as a celebration of trans-Atlantic enterprise, 'his centrality between America and Africa', in a scene where 'the rocky New England shoreline' lies off 'the brig Traveller's bow' with 'the palm-lined West African coast' to her stern.[29] One might want to supplement Thomas's brief account with a consideration of the small picturesque figures inhabiting the indeterminate in-between landscape at the bottom of this striking image. Such an account might imagine how they might be able to respond to the arrival of the brig *Traveller* and how they might view her captain and crew. But the figure of Captain Cuffe himself in fashionable silhouette perhaps best represents the story of his self-fashioning as we have seen it from his own pen and that of others, as well as from the loaded vantage-point of his entry into the port of Liverpool: a monochrome blanking out of one side of his inheritance in favour of a patrilinear trans-Atlantic idealism.

NOTES

1. See *Captain Paul Cuffe's Logs and Letters 1808-1817: A Black Quaker's "Voice from within the Veil"*, ed., Rosalind Cobb Wiggins with an introduction by Rhett S. Jones (Washington DC: Howard UP, 1996), p. 132.
2. Lamont D. Thomas, *Paul Cuffe: Black Entrepreneur and Pan-Africanist* (Urbana: U of Illinois P, 1988), originally published in 1986 as *Rise to Be a People: A Biography of Paul Cuffe*; Sheldon Harris, *Paul Cuffe: Black America and the African Return* (New York: Simon and Schuster, 1972); John Stauffer, 'In the Shadow of a Dream: White Abolitionists and Race', in *Proceedings of the Fifth Annual Gilder Lehrman Center International Conference at Yale University*, 'Collective Degradation: Slavery and the Construction of Race', 7-8 November 2003 (New Haven, Connecticut: Yale UP), pp. 7-9.
3. See Paul Cuffe, *Brief Account of the Settlement and Present Situation of the Colony of Sierra Leone in Africa* (New York: Samuel Wood, 1812).
4. See Jane Longmore, 'Civic Liverpool 1660-1800', in *Liverpool 800: Culture, Character and History*, ed., John Belchem (Liverpool: Liverpool UP, 2008), pp. 113-70, esp. 131-135; David Richardson, 'Slavery and Bristol's "Golden Age"', *Slavery and Abolition* 26:1 April (2005) 38; Roger Anstey and P.E.H. Hair, eds, *Liverpool, the African Slave Trade,*

and Abolition: Essays to Illustrate Current Knowledge and Research, vol. 2 (Historic Society of Lancashire and Cheshire, Occasional Series, 1976), esp. pp. 60-122, 126-56.

5. *Edinburgh Review*, XXXVI, August 1811, p. 321.

6. *Memoir of Captain Paul Cuffee, a man of colour*. Written expressly for, and originally printed in, the *Liverpool Mercury* (Liverpool: Printed and sold by Egerton Smith and Co., and D. Eaton, High Holburn, London, 1811).

7. See Harris, *Paul Cuffe: Black America and the African Return*; Thomas, *Paul Cuffe: Black Entrepreneur and Pan-Africanist*, esp. pp. 46-107; *Logs and Letters*, esp. pp. 97-248, 325-488; David Kazanjian, 'Mercantile Exchanges, Mercantilist Enclosures: Racial Capitalism in the Black Mariner Narratives of Venture Smith and John Jea', *New Centennial Review*, 3.1 (2003) 147-78.

8. Simon Schama, *Rough Crossings: Britain, the Slaves and the American Revolution* (London: BBC Books, 2005), pp. 9, 388-91, 394.

9. *Logs and Letters*, p. 80. Cuffe writes, 'And as I am of the African race I feel myself interested for them'.

10. *Liverpool Mercury; or Commercial, Literary and Political Herald*, Friday 9 August 1811. See also: *The Times*, Friday, 2 August 1811, p. 3, col. E.

11. *Liverpool Mercury*, 9 August 1811.

12. William Cowper, 'The Negro's Lament' (1788).

13. *Memoir of Captain Paul Cuffee, A Man of Colour: To which is subjoined The Epistle of the Society of Sierra Leone, In Africa; &c.* (York: Printed by C. Peacock for W. Alexander, 1811), p. 22.

14. Benjamin Seebohm, ed., *Memoirs of the Life and Gospel Labours of Stephen Grellet*, 2 vols ([1860]; Philadelphia: Edward Marsh, 1874), I, p. 171.

15. *Logs and Letters*, p. 343.

16. *Logs and Letters*, p. 121.

17. *Logs and Letters*, p. 78.

18. *Logs and Letters*, pp. 80, 120, 343.

19. *Logs and Letters*, p. 103.

20. *Logs and Letters*, p. 437.

21. *Logs and Letters*, p. 276.

22. *Logs and Letters*, p. 192.

23. *Logs and Letters*, p. 343.

24. *Logs and Letters*, p. 217.

25. *Logs and Letters*, p. 213.

26. Peter Williams Jun., *A Discourse Delivered On the Death of Captain Paul Cuffee Before the New York African Institution in The African Methodist Episcopal Zion Church, October 21, 1817 by Peter Williams, Jun., A Man of Colour*, published by request of some members of that Institution. (New York and London: Simon and Schuster: printed for W. Alexander, 1818), pp. v, 9, 17, 23, 24, 10, 29.

27. *Narrative of the Life and Adventures of Paul Cuffe, A Pequot Indian: During Thirty Years Spent at Sea, and in Travelling in Foreign Lands* (Vernon: Printed by Horace N. Bill, 1839), p. 1.

28. See Harris, *Paul Cuffe: Black America and the African Return* pp. 15, 37 and Henry Noble Sherwood, 'Paul Cuffe', *Journal of Negro History*, VIII (April 1923), p. 163. Harris describes Cuffe as 'vacillat[ing] between his Negro and his Indian origins' and declares that his 'racial ambiguity was genuine' (p. 37).

29. Thomas, *Paul Cuffe: Black Entrepreneur and Pan-Africanist*, p. vi.

The Words To Tell Them

DINESH ALLIRAJAH

You approach from one of the streets, something-Dale, the names of which you once learned but have forgotten again. Each one is tributary to the main road; and that, an intersection of the city's major ring road – in fact, a crescent, as it's the river that completes the circle. The dual carriageway coughs and splutters in suitably urban tones but, just one street called something-Dale away, and you're in an English suburb with salt on the breeze. This is where you came, and you carried the description of its coordinates in your head to take back and recite like a poem until you realized: this is where you are.

Your finger chases a moment's moisture across your lips. It glides at first but, as the lips return to their previous dryness, the movement becomes more of a stumble and drag. With each step, you develop a more intense awareness of what your body is doing, as though the skin, nerves, muscles and skeleton have all been picked up and shuffled, then left to sort themselves back into place for this short walk to your house. Your toenails feel like they're having their first encounter with socks; your knees appear to be questioning their design and flexing to sit down when the rest of the body is upright. You know you'll soon be sitting down in your house, with your wife and your son, but you're compelled to retreat, back through time and place, from that conversation. You need to find another way for your words to reach them today. For the first time in your life, you're going to have to search for the words.

A page of a newspaper blows past, briefly reflecting sunlight from the gutter in a way that catches your eye like a camera flash. You look down and you can see words, bouncing up from the road, on to the pavement and back. You make shovel hands to pick them up and scout around for a box to put them in, a wooden crate such as might be packed with coconuts, green and shuddering with the weight of their water. Here, on this English street corner, you could hand the coconuts out to passers-by so they could cool their throats while you stood on the upturned box and regaled them with passages from the *Tamil Culture* journal, smuggled in from Madras. Now the words are finding you, faster than your eyes can shut them out. They're on street signs, car registrations, leaflets for takeaways in neighbours' letterboxes. There are the slogans in a suppressed tongue, laced with wonky translations of Marx and Trotsky, that saw you jettisoned from your homeland. You can make out the muttered conversations that secured the passage out to anywhere; there's the slang, newly acquired when you arrived. And then you can see the letters to your first love, spelling out why this icy port, as near the Arctic as makes no difference, could be the shade in which to grow a family before transplanting it back home to catch the sun.

A bedroom window shuts just late enough for you to hear but not recognize the music whose volume has been turned up inside. You grab the cartilage of those few chords you manage to hear and add them to the other sediments and specimens of music you've retained over the years. This rhythmic clamour displaces the words you've just found, in much the same way that your formative political struggle, the one you came here to expand, gave way to new passions once you set foot on these streets chaperoning Penny Lane. You found you could wait at a bus-stop and be inside a hit record, and the bus would take you to blues parties, concert halls, and soul basements. You learned to wear polo neck jumpers and stand at bars, with a haircut modelled after Tony Gomez, the keyboardist from The Foundations, your countryman, and you learned to accept each mistaken identity. You learned to agree with stoned young men about how cool everything always was; you learned to strike up conversations with the girl in the band, or the one behind the record shop counter, or the one on the dance floor, around whom the club fanned like the Ted Heath Band behind Lita Roza. You stocked up on it all but, note by note, you gave most of it away. You put jazz into the names of your two children; you fell in love with a dance floor siren and used up all your seduction serenades; you left the heartbreak songs folded up in the drawers and cupboards of the family home you abandoned. You try to hum what's left, and the coughing surges back and envelops all other sound, as it usually does. However, when you reach your house, you're pleased to note that you're still trying to hum.

The house, semi-detached, sits at the other end of a demure front garden. Other gardens and driveways along this road are busier, with cars and trees and flowers; a pair of Chinese lions guarding one front door; basketball hoops and water features. Your garden has grass. There used to be a tree and, when you sit on the low wall separating the grass from the road, you're in the shadow of its former branches. When you stand up, you can pluck its once-blossom. You stand on the grass, and time crumples. Your head feels midday heat but you hug your chest against the evening chill; your shoes and then your socks sense morning dew. You look down to where you've just been treading. The grass remains flattened in your footprint for a few seconds before flexing, curling, and then springing back into place. You take heavier steps towards the house, pushing your feet down until they feel embedded in the soil. Your soil. This is where you came, from a pebble in the Indian Ocean to one of a cluster at the edge of the Atlantic, to skim across the soil, learn the names of the streets, stock up on the music and take it all back. But this soil is now what belongs to you.

You stand with your feet in the soil and watch the house fall like a scattered photograph album. You see scrawled captions detailing inconsequential change: 'New house: front door.' 'Front door: new coat of paint.' 'Bay window: double-glazing installed!' The window once had Venetian blinds; at one time, roller blinds. The photographs spin past your head. Now there's a net curtain obscuring a clear view into the living room but get very close to the glass and you can cast a shadow on the net. Within that, you can see your reflection and, through your reflection, you can look inside your house.

There are no photographs visible on the walls of the living room, nor on the sideboards and dressers outspanning two dark brown leather armchairs, a coffee table and wooden IKEA storage chest with its lid off. In the middle of the floor, though, in between the eyes of your reflected face, there is a picture of two women, clutched together in an embrace, both convulsed in sobbing. You step back. Worm-turned topsoil shakes itself back onto the ground from the soles of your shoes. When you return to the window, you allow the objects inside the living room to take shape again. The two women are still there but now all they're sharing is a chilly restraint. The older woman is standing up and retrieving something from the storage chest, a grey box designed to hold a card index, which she passes to the younger woman, seated in one of the leather armchairs. You take a heavy blink. It reminds you that what you're watching is really nothing more substantial than a reflection of your own two eyes, but you feel you could almost touch these shapes now, and you continue to watch.

The box rattles as Chan, the younger woman, places it on her knees. She finds the noise mildly startling, but the act of opening the box – left thumb lifting the lid just enough for the right index finger to squeeze into the gap and flick the lid up and back – is familiar and comfortable. The box contains no photographs either but, again, as Chan sifts prickly mounds of lapel badges through her fingers, she imagines a snapshot, propped up in the inside of the box's lid. A teenage girl is pictured, wearing a large black suit jacket, three-quarter length blue trousers appropriate for work in a paddy field, white socks and Dr Marten shoes. The girl is holding up a photocopy of the South African Rand *Daily Mail*'s front page. The paper's columns are daubed with black stripes and blocks. The girl's hair is shaved at the sides but it tumbles from the top like a black yucca plant, and shades her eyes. This contrasts with Chan, whose hair is scraped back with bronze highlights and held in a short ponytail. She nonetheless makes a brushing motion in front of her own eyes and then picks up a badge, identical to one in the photograph on the girl's right sleeve, the sleeve held across her chest as she points to one of the black stripes in the newspaper. The badge, a pink disc the size of a yoghurt pot lid, reads, 'How Dare You Presume I'm Heterosexual?'

For a moment, before she looks up from the box of badges, Chan can see another picture. It shows her with her partner Paul and a group of friends around a dinner table. The dinner table is in their house; not this house, the one she's sitting in now. The house isn't in this city and, though it's not really all that far away – they're both in Britain, after all, which she's always liked to call a pebble at the edge of the Atlantic – the distance has been multiplied by time. She tastes the water on the dinner table, feels Paul's arm around the back of her chair, and hears the laughs of her friends as she tells them, 'But, of course, I *was* heterosexual!'

She looks up, and the picture vanishes, replaced by the sight of the older woman. Having sat back in her armchair after giving Chan the box, Alice has now got to her feet again, smoothes the hem of her black sweater over slim hips. She excuses herself in her own house and heads towards the kitchen. Chan notices Alice's simple jewellery as her stiff movements haul her across the room. There's a smart silver bracelet tapping at her right wrist bone when she tugs at her sweater and, on the left wrist, a softer, non-metallic band, a surprising bright yellow against her dark clothes.

Chan has mounted more of the badges against the inside of the lid, holding it from the back so it stays upright and the badges don't fall. The names of bands appear on some badges, in constipated versions of the logos seen on record sleeves and tour posters. There are some images or symbols: the inverted trident of CND, a picture of Martin Luther King; another of the young, chubby, and bearded Nelson Mandela; a map of England, Scotland, and Wales clubbing a map of Ireland; the letter A intersecting a circle at five points. Then there are the slogans: Solidarno; Rock Against Racism; If Voting Changed Anything, They'd Abolish It; A Woman Needs A Man Like A Fish Needs A Bike; Make Love Not War; Don't Vote – It Only Encourages Them; Coal Not Dole; Jobs Not Bombs; Legalise It.

The girl in the photograph is wearing several of these badges. Chan can count each of the pins that might leave slender dimples in the skin when pressed to her body in a hug. But Chan isn't hugging the girl. She's not even holding the oversize suit jacket, and there is no photograph. She is just clutching a box, and even that is set aside when Alice returns with two mugs of coffee. As if conscious of its prescribed role, the coffee warms both pairs of hands as it passes between them.

Chan twitches a smile for Alice's benefit, gazes into the open storage chest at cassettes, diaries, books and clothes that trace the outline of a teenage girl, and speaks. 'Did he keep – hasn't Charlie got anything of his in there?'

Alice follows her gaze. 'No, well, you see, Charlie always – we get to see your brother so … much … more … um … than – he doesn't, didn't need to keep anything –'

'OK,' Chan says, swiftly. She can see that a badge has appeared on Alice's chest, with the first letter of each word capitalized, so it's more a slogan than a statement: He Kept Charlie.

Chan looks down at her own lapel, and there is a button badge, hurriedly pinned so it's upside down, and she can read, 'Because Charlie's Captain Compromise'. And, on the rectangular mirror badge further down, 'Because He Thinks You Look Like Helen Mirren'.

Chan ignores the coaster Alice has fetched from the kitchen and places her mug on the newspaper that sits crookedly on the coffee table. The *Mail*'s headline is covered by a black strip. The coffee's heat causes the strip to curl at the edge and peel back, revealing the words, 'Because At 19 He Just Admired The Old Man's Pulling Power'. Below the banner, the sub-heading reveals itself: 'Because A Horny Little Rat-Boy Will Forgive A Sexy Blonde Anything, Even Destroying A Family.' Chan closes her eyes, forms her finger and thumb into a chevron to rub the eyelids so that, when she opens her eyes again, the words have gone. Nevertheless, she can see that Alice is also staring at the newspaper headline. Chan twitches another smile and rejoins the mutual silence.

You whisper the names of these two women, 'Alice' and 'Chan', your second wife and your daughter, each of whom has only ever been 'she' and 'her' to the other. You think about the word, *estrangement*, and how clever it was of the English to make it sound French. You remember how Joel Grey pronounced '*étrangers*' in *Cabaret*, and you look for strangers in your living room. But you see the woman whose arches and curves and lines you could trace in the air with your finger so accurately, people would walk up and shake the empty space by the hand. You look across to the woman whose broad nose, and furrowed brow, and mouth always on the cusp of an argument or a withering punchline, are your own. She gazes at the box of badges and it is with your eyes. She takes a small sip of coffee but needs a large gulp to help it down, and your Adam's apple hums like the rim of a wine glass rubbed with a moist finger.

The badges give a hushed rattle. Chan sees that her hands are vibrating, and she tries to chase the tremors away with a swift, sharp flick. She sees that Alice, too, is stretching out her fingers, each hand taking its turn to massage the tips of the other, and she can see Alice's yellow band more clearly now on her left wrist. Chan's words then come out in a gasp. Her surprise – that she's even making conversation – is headline-bold in her voice.

'Is that for cancer?' She grabs her own wrist to mime the band.

Alice flexes her wrist so the band hangs loosely, only in contact with the skin at her pulse point. 'No,' she says, her voice slowing to a halt around the 'o'. She examines the wristband as if this is the first time its presence has been brought to her attention. 'It's…well, it's *against* cancer.'

There's a moment before Alice smiles; twenty years and another moment before Chan gives her a broad smile back. Alice takes that, and places it in the storage chest from IKEA.

The glass comes into sudden contact with your nose so you emit two stubby jets of air, momentary imprints on the window. The front door is unlocked, a turn of its handle enough to take you inside, and your key points uselessly forward. You place it on the little table by the door, alongside the spare set.

Another door takes you into the room where Alice is standing with one hand pressed into her waist. It's her model pose, the one you'd always stand back and enjoy and then do your best to dismember: sliding your hand into hers, burrowing into her neck so she hangs her head to the side, the tip of her nose touching your forehead. Then you'd lick the neck, grab at the breast, reach between the legs and rub, so she'd be forced to slap your naughty fingers, and peel away and once more get to be the Ice Blonde they all watched on the dance floor and said you'd never melt, but your body would still be warming hers after she'd crossed the room. Today, there's no stunted attempt at seduction. You do, though, grab her left wrist but you do so in order to find the wristband you'd seen her wear through the window. There is no wristband. Not yet, you realize. You work a finger underneath the gold watch strap that's spent each day there since it became your first Christmas present to her. For a moment – for ten seconds; you watch each one pass – you both look at the time. Eventually, you let go of Alice's wrist and your heads turn towards the figure sitting in one of the armchairs.

'Hello son,' you say to Charlie. Your voice drops like a marble into a bottle bank. Your eyes dart about the room. There's no sign of Chan, other than in a photograph on the sideboard, in which she's sitting at a dinner table with her partner, Paul, and they're laughing. You realize that the other shape in the room was Charlie. It was always Charlie. Ever since the end of your first marriage, the only other shape in the room with you and Alice has been Charlie.

'OK, Dad?'

Charlie is dressed, here and now as always, for the office. It's not simply the collar and tie: it's the flexing of the tie's knot, gearing up for a PowerPoint presentation of whatever he needs to tell you; it's the way he sits with just the one buttock on the seat cushion and one eye on the Blackberry, hot-desking you. Your son folds his newspaper and tosses it on to the coffee table. You nod and smile at him but your eyes are drawn to the paper's masthead, the lettering recognizable but alien. You make a mental check back over decades of oaths and New Year resolutions: there's a copy of the *Daily Mail* in your house. It's not here by accident. It belongs to your son, Charlie. He was named after Charlie Parker, whom the *Mail* would pillory now for his drug use or ignore for his music, whichever would be more damaging. You look back at your darling intruder. He straightens his tie again and you remember the pride you have in the hard worker he's always been; you marvel at the way he slots so securely into place in this land. He's the tree whose blossom would once have perfumed the grass in front of the house; he's your blossom, apple-cheeked, office-ready and reading the *Daily Mail*.

Chan would have started the fight by now. You named her for Parker's soul mate, Chan Richardson, because you thought she would love music and musicians but also stand up to them. She'd be standing now, brushing aside Alice and Charlie's complaints that this was no time for arguments about the *Daily Mail* – arguments about politics, arguments at all – anymore.

You watch her as she refuses to back down. She's there in front of you, jabbing, punching the headline. She doesn't look like the woman in the photograph on the sideboard. She's younger and the hair is different, darker; it shades her eyes. She's wearing a black jacket and there are badges on its lapels and sleeves.

You need a badge now, or a newspaper headline. You need to grab hold of the *Mail* and tear out the letters to spell what you have to tell them.

'So…?' Charlie leaves a space for you to speak.

You look for the footprints on the carpet where your daughter has been standing and you realize that Alice has hold of your hand again but, this time, she's helping you to your seat.

Reading as 'social glue'? Book Groups, Multiculture, and the *Small Island Read 2007*

DANIELLE FULLER & JAMES PROCTER

> Well, it's [*Small Island*] linking people who come here isn't it, it's their history isn't it, their personal history. So it's – we've all got connections to other cultures, particularly in this city [Liverpool], and it's like a bridge. (Linda, 'Liverpool Reads' participant) [1]

> Um, 'social glue' I think was the word that we, we came up with, the words that we came up with, that we thought it was a, a kind of social glue. And the difficulty with *Small Island* was, because it's not, umm, necessarily a crossover book. (Beccy Jones, Bluecoat Arts Centre, Liverpool) [2]

In 2007 Andrea Levy's award-winning novel, *Small Island* (2004), was selected for the UK's largest-ever mass-reading event. What cultural work was the novel assumed to perform by the organizers, sponsors, and institutions associated with this event? Were they in tension with the ways that actual readers responded to the novel? Can a fictional bestseller that evokes the *Windrush* generation encourage contemporary readers to share, or even resolve, not only their different perspectives on *Small Island*, but also their perspectives on cultural difference? How should we understand the relationship between a piece of internationally-acclaimed, metropolitan fiction, and a local readership in the North West of England? Focusing on Liverpool, which was one of the four city sites of *Small Island Read 2007*, our essay explores these questions by drawing on selected data gathered from two large-scale collaborative research projects funded by the AHRC, 'Beyond the Book' and 'Devolving Diasporas'.[3] The material we analyse includes official documents, press releases, and statements issued by several agencies involved in the event. We also consider recorded focus group and book group conversations with a variety of UK readers, the majority of whom live in Liverpool.

Liverpool is a multiracial port city in which more than 60 languages are spoken. With a current population of 436,100, the city is home to Europe's longest-established Chinese community,[4] but its ties with the peoples of the African diaspora are even older because of the city's historical (and infamous) role within the transatlantic slave trade. As Linda suggests in the opening quotation, many contemporary Liverpudlians have historical, familial or social 'connections' to more than one cultural community dwelling within the city limits. However, the multicultural demographic of Liverpool is rarely signified within popular representations of the city either within or outside the UK. For example, the celebratory discourses of arrival and beginning, that are ritually associated with the London-centred narrative of the *SS Empire Windrush* docking at Tilbury in June 1948 with its cargo of 492 West Indian emigrants, consistently overshadow the race riots that took place in Liverpool just two months later. As James Procter has argued elsewhere, 'these disturbances, concerning the large numbers of black seamen who had come to settle in the city during the war, signal the presence of alternative beginnings and earlier arrivals.'[5] At stake here is an elision that is both historical and geographical: if, within the symbolic discourses of multiculturalism, London remains an emphatic epicentre, this partly depends upon a recurring sense of the north and other regional settings as being *beyond* migration and diaspora. Thus, Liverpool's international image has, until very recently, been primarily secured by the city's association with successful football clubs, The Beatles, and working-class poverty. Such representations are never far away from national nostalgias about local community, neighbourhood, and social solidarity, invocations of which often refer, either implicitly or explicitly, to homogenous 'white' populations. These kinds of contradictions between Liverpool as at once *prior* to the Windrush yet peripheral to diaspora, were, we shall see, played out during *Small Island Reads 2007*.

The Liverpool-based co-ordinators situated in 'The Reader' office had previously organized two successful city-wide reading events of their own ('Liverpool Reads') and, because of their extensive work with socially and economically marginalized groups, were fully aware of divisions within their city community.[6] As Beccy Jones notes in the epigraph above, and as Jane Davis, founder of 'The Reader' organization, has often remarked in press statements, the concept of a city-wide event favoured by the 'Liverpool Reads' committee was underwritten by the idea of shared reading as a type of 'social glue'.[7] This conceptualization implies a desire to bring people across the city of Liverpool together by offering the common ground of a single book, perhaps with the aim of healing those social divisions. However, as we demonstrate in this essay, these well-intentioned goals are at odds with some of the aims and structures shaping the larger-scale *Small Island Read* project, and also with the logic of dominant discourses of multiculturalism operating in the UK. For instance, what kind of erasures and assumptions might be involved in prescribing a London-produced, metropolitan novel to a 'local' Liverpudlian readership despite that city's own long and rich history of postwar Caribbean and black British writing? In order to address this question, our essay will make a distinction between the rhetoric of multiculturalism – as it is sanctioned at an official level, and was reproduced in the publicity statements around *Small Island Reads 2007* – and Paul Gilroy's notion of 'multiculture', which describes informal, vernacular expressions of cross-cultural connection that are arguably closer to the local readings of *Small Island* considered in the final section of the essay.

Local sites/national structures: situating the tensions of *Small Island Reads*

We have quoted above Beccy Jones's statement that *Small Island* was not a 'crossover book'. Given our concerns in this essay, it is tempting to interpret her phrase as referring to a book's capacity to appeal to different cultural communities, thereby supplying the 'social glue' that might foster stronger relationships among the city's diverse groups. However, Jones, who was part of the original 'Liverpool Reads' committee, is making a more nuanced point which is that book selection is key to the programme achieving any kind of connection among the city's readers. She notes here that the choice of an adult novel for the 2007 'Liverpool Reads' represented a deviation from the programme's preferred genre. 'Liverpool Reads 2006', for example, focused upon *Millions* by the Liverpudlian author, Frank Cotterell Boyce, a novel intended primarily for school-aged children, but one which can also be enjoyed by adults.[8] *Millions* is also the only 'Liverpool Reads' selection to date to have been written by a local writer, from which we can infer that celebrating Liverpool's literary talent is not necessarily an aim of the programme. This situation is, however, typical of many 'One Book, One Community' city-wide reading initiatives in the UK and in North America. While not all programmes share Liverpool's emphasis on involving schools and young people from diverse communities, organizers frequently select books because they articulate themes, issues, and ideas that are pertinent to the inhabitants of a locale and, crucially, because they have the potential to appeal to male and female readers across different age groups.[9] Since 'Liverpool Reads 2007' was part of a larger-scale programme – *Small Island Read 2007* – the selection of Levy's novel was not even made by the Liverpool organizers but by Bristol Cultural Development Partnership, the team who have successfully run Bristol's 'Great Reading Adventure' since 2003.

Nevertheless, the choice of a mainstream, best-selling migrant narrative with a predominantly London setting might seem odd, given that the partner cities in *Small Island Read* were Bristol, Glasgow, Hull and Liverpool. Arguably, the choice reinforces an ideology that posits London as the apotheosis of the culturally sophisticated 'multicultural' metropolis. However, as we shall see below, many of the participating Liverpudlian readers move with consummate and apparently untroubled ease between local, metropolitan, and national landscapes in their accounts.

While the selection of Levy's novel plays into discursive tensions about the location of 'multicultural Britain', further contradictions arise from the ambiguous private/public situation and political efficacy of another site materialized by *Small Island Read*, namely, the book group. If the image of the solitary reader has been historically dominant since medieval times, the emergence of book groups during the nineteenth century suggests a dramatic alternative to commonsense notions of reading as a private, individual, silent, and cognitive act.[10] Moreover, the phenomenal success of book groups in contemporary Britain, Canada, and the USA indicates that many readers pursue reading as a social, communal, public and conversational activity. Even if they do not always result in a meeting of minds, book groups involve a social gathering, a physical, face-to-face encounter, or a virtual, online meeting that ensures no reader is an island.[11] Book group discussion is typically intersectional, involving processes such as cross-cultural identification, and the sharing of perspectives and interpretations in a process that is both collaborative and dialogic. Certainly, there is evidence in the groups we have worked with that book discussions can create a meeting place for intergenerational understanding, or construct an ideological common ground by articulating and reflecting upon previously internalized values and attitudes about 'race', class, and gender. The identity work that readers undertake in the act of shared reading can even involve making connections among these 'categories', as well as interrogating how and why those categories have been formalized through educational institutions, societal norms, economic structures and the legacies of British imperial histories.

In other ways, however, the book group formation seems stubbornly resistant to the kinds of cross-cultural meeting we might wish to associate with progressive political action. Book groups tend to divide along the lines of ethnicity and gender, if not generation, so that relatively homogenous gatherings (for example, all-male and all-female groups) predominate. Equally, there is evidence to suggest that book groups often exert exclusionary practices, deterring or being suspicious of new members.[12] Given their typical demographics, the political limits of contemporary book groups as sites of ideological transformation might seem glaringly obvious. The shared reading of *Small Island* in book groups offers no guarantees that any kind of transformative meeting will occur. Nevertheless, book group readers together constitute a large and all too easily neglected interpretive community for Levy's text. We believe that ignoring this reading community would itself be a politically irresponsible act. In what follows, we offer a critique of the *Small Island Read* event by approaching it from two perspectives: first, in terms of how the groups were depicted in official documents and statements (that is, in methodological terms), we investigate *Small Island Read* from 'above' and from the standpoint of its organizing agencies; and, second, we consider how actual readers on the ground responded to the text in group conversations and interviews.

Small Island Read: rhetoric and representation

Small Island Read 2007 was the largest mass-reading event ever held in the UK. Running from 11 January to 31 March 2007, it involved the distribution of 50,000 free copies of Andrea Levy's novel, along with 80,000 copies of a glossy A5 readers' guide. It generated 100 separate events (including library talks, book group discussions, competitions, exhibitions), and 60 school workshops. Drawing on earlier mass-reading initiatives in Liverpool and Bristol, and integrating Glasgow and Hull as new partner cities, the event was centred around, but moved beyond, four locations with clear links to the slave trade.[13] The declared aims of the event were as follows:

- To develop standards of literacy through the promotion of reading.
- To stimulate new forms of creativity inspired by the reading experience.
- To use reading to facilitate learning about the past.
- To bring diverse communities together through the act of reading and thereby foster a sense of shared identity.[14]

Within this official agenda, the book is asked to operate as a hinge between 'the past' (slavery and its abolition; postwar immigration) and the present (contemporary multicultural diversity). As the funders articulated it in a joint statement: 'Remembering the victims of the slave trade is essential in everyone's lives. Just as important is celebrating the diversity of the modern city.'[15] Second, and more precisely, it is the reader and 'the act of reading' *Small Island* that is envisaged as a kind of pull string, capable of drawing diverse reading communities together and 'foster[ing] a shared identity'.

This goal of historical and communal cohesion is perhaps most clearly and coherently embodied in the visual archive housed on the *Small Island Read 2007* website, where dozens of photographs depicting assembled readers serve to perform and stage the act of reading the novel.[16] The collected subjects holding or surrounding copies of the book appear to personify the diversity and multiculturalism which the sponsors of the mass-reading event would like *Small Island* to perform. The book as a material artefact comes to represent a physical meeting place, drawing communities of difference together. Most notable here is the exclusive emphasis on the depiction of inclusiveness and diversity with reference to ethnicity but also through the combination and juxtaposition of different classes, generations, and sexes. Glaswegian bus drivers are depicted brandishing free paperback editions of *Small Island* alongside a photograph of uniformed schoolgirls with copies of the same text. Collectively these images concretize the slogan adopted by many of the community-based reading programmes involved in the project: 'reading as social glue'.

To what extent are these images and the rhetoric undermined or contradicted by the event itself? The evaluation report tells us that the majority of readers were middle class, 72 per cent were female, 91 per cent white. There is nothing particularly surprising about this. Indeed, the notable homogeneity of the reading group as an Anglo-American social formation means that these statistics point to a *relative* diversity. Certainly there was a concerted and laudable effort on the part of the event organizers to bring together different participants. Among the events programmed for *Small Island Read/* 'Liverpool Reads', for example, were a reading group at the Caribbean community centre; a creative writing project with young Somalis; a reading group at the Asylum Link; a Youth Project run by refugee artists, and a drama project with young people from the Yemeni Arabic community. Nevertheless, these initiatives were fraught with problems and ultimately highlighted some of the limitations of the mass-read project as a community-wide activity. They include the difficulties involved in providing sufficient numbers of English for Speakers of Other Languages (ESOL) support workers; the non-availability of *Small Island* in languages other than English; issues of illiteracy among some groups within the city, and racist remarks in reading group discussions, which threatened the possibility of cross-racial reading groups.

In this context, events like *Small Island Read* provide a glimpse of the limitations of state-sanctioned multiculturalism. The main national sponsors of *Small Island Read* were Arts Council England and the Heritage Lottery Fund. Viewed sceptically, the images and rhetoric outlined above might be said to 'tick boxes' to secure financial support from sponsors with a public commitment to corporate multiculturalism, and/or to demonstrate that the money has been 'well spent'.[17] From this perspective, the photographic images of *Small Island* as a meeting place of cultural diversity operate as 'proof' of an easily achieved and celebratory multiculturalism, and as a visual shorthand that conceals the challenges and contingencies of actually-existing 'multiculture'. In *After Empire*, Paul Gilroy uses the term 'multiculture', as opposed to multiculturalism, to describe the kind of spontaneous, precarious, and provisional cross-cultural interactions he sees emerging in contemporary British culture.[18] Multiculture is not something that can be sanctioned or prescribed from above. Instead Gilroy conceptualizes it as erupting erratically in the vernacular formations of everyday life. If the actual readers of *Small Island* cannot be said to read entirely outside the more programmatic logic of the event's official rhetoric (a logic which suggests reading *Small Island* necessarily achieves 'diversity'), they offer a more complex picture of cultural *reception* (as both hermeneutics and hospitality) that is arguably closer to multiculture than multiculturalism.

Meeting-places: reading *Small Island* together

While some of the readers we worked with found the multi-voiced narrative of *Small Island* difficult to follow and an obstacle to their initial engagement with the text, many were pulled into the plot and the world of Levy's novel through the characters of Queenie, Bernard, Gilbert and Hortense. Identification with these fictional figures, or lack of it, makes up a substantial part of the talk on and around *Small Island* that we have analysed so far. As one white reader noted of the novel during a focus group discussion in Liverpool:

> It just adds to the actual history doesn't it, you know to to read from a human perspective I suppose … It adds humanity, it adds um – you know you, you can read about things and say, 'Oh that's so awful' … and it, and it, or something, you know – but to actually read from a – about things from a human perspective, of a character that's been created, then I think you can be, well, truly moved, in a way that just reading about the history – and it can be when you read about the history as well but it just adds that extra humanity.[19]

This reader reminds us of the extent to which the individual voices of the novel serve to profoundly personalize the historical narrative in ways that encourage readerly identification. (Perhaps the centrality of character in *Small Island* is one reason for the novel's popularity with book groups and other non-academic readers.) On one level, the connection between the novel and 'history' seems to reiterate the framing of the novel for the *Small Island Read* event, which contextualized *Small Island* in terms of the history of British slavery and postwar immigration. However, this reader also suggests that engaging with Levy's fictional work involves *more than* 'just reading about the history' with its dispassionate or merely gestural empathy: 'Oh that's so awful.' Reading *Small Island*-as-fiction, this reader suggests, has the capacity to elicit a personal and human response, to be 'truly moved'. If such an emotive account might be said to mystify the actual identity-work being done through the act of reading, it also captures the more elusive, less accountable, and programmatic perspectives that have emerged in the recorded conversations around *Small Island*.

Below is a conversation between a group of women readers, also based in Liverpool, as they reflect approvingly upon the 'realistic' and 'detailed' descriptions of Queenie and Hortense. In common with women's book groups featured in other scholarly studies, these readers privilege a mimetic reading practice in order to find points of identification with fictional characters, and with their own lives.[20] As their discussion proceeds, these women admire Hortense's self-presentation as a respectable, educated woman who, at first, does not appear to notice the everyday racism that she encounters in 1940s London. Within their analysis of Hortense's attitudes and behaviour, class is foregrounded until one reader suggests how the experience of migration might produce disappointment in a newly arrived immigrant through the disillusion of expectations and desires that have been founded on (colonialist?) stereotypes of the receiving culture:

> S4 She's aspiring to better things isn't she? She hasn't really got anything to be that way about but she's aspiring to live a better life and have better things isn't she?
> S1 She's very judgemental though isn't she? Everybody else you know does everything wrong
> S2 I think I might be like her if I went to live there somewhere in Africa and I've got my idea of Africans busy eating mangos in the sunshine (laughter)[21]

In their efforts to make sense of Hortense's actions and opinions, these readers move towards a creative re-reading of the text, imagining themselves into an analogous situation where cultural and racial difference is handled through stereotypes, while remaining sensitive to their material effects. (Elsewhere they discuss Hortense coming up against institutionalized racism, for instance.) It is not easy to 'read off' from this conversation a positive encounter between (white, Liverpudlian) reader and (West Indian) character, assuming we could know what such an encounter might look like. For example, there is no obvious attempt by these readers to distance themselves from or to denounce racial stereotypes but instead a more risky parodying of them which, depending on how you read it, stresses the absurdity of stereotype (which provokes knowing laughter) or reinforces it (by provoking ignorant laughter). Within a long established book group such as this, where trust among members is firm and readers feel able to voice their opinions safely, it nevertheless appears possible to activate the text as a meeting-place for critical reflection, with some readers approving of Hortense's personality, others disapproving, others changing their minds in an open, dialogic, and ultimately inconclusive conversation.

Transcripts from other group discussions of Levy's novel, and from focus groups with readers in and beyond Liverpool, suggest that a common element of reader response is a consideration of what, if anything, has changed about race relations and racist attitudes in the UK.[22] For a reading group in Chepstow, discussion about the title and its possible reference to 'small-mindedness' prompted this type of response. Meanwhile, Anne, a white middle-aged woman in a Liverpool focus group, was particularly affected by Gilbert's experiences of racism:

> [Gilbert] eventually is stationed over in Britain, and at that point you get the, sort of, the interaction with the white British and the different reactions. Again some of them really, embarrassingly, shaming I thought, from my point of view being, you know, a white British person, and … I, I found it very difficult at times to read it and accept that it still goes on in some ways. This is it, all, all through the book you get the, sort of, this is what happened then. In some ways it's not so different to now, um, in terms of attitude, very often.[23]

Within the context of a racially mixed focus group, it is possible that Anne may have felt compelled to offer this self-aware commentary in order to demonstrate her own tolerance. However, Anne's discomfort and her recognition that racism 'still goes on in some ways' was not atypical.

Readers also made connections between slavery and the present-day use of child labour as well as relating the discrimination suffered by Gilbert and Hortense to the introduction of citizenship tests. They also discussed the representation of new immigrants and asylum seekers in tabloid newspapers as evidence that many attitudes have not shifted, and engaged in discussion of the economic basis of empire and colonial expansion, discussions which segued into considerations of outsourcing to Indian call centres. Admittedly, most of the readers in our studies knew that the selection of *Small Island* was intended to coincide with the bicentenary of the Abolition of the Slave Trade, but this factor suggests that framing the community-wide read in this way helped to foreground the contemporary relevance of the novel and thus prompted readers to use a fictional story set in the past to debate current political and social issues. Kerry, an African-Caribbean woman in her late thirties, recognized the potential of this text to unsettle racist assumptions within what Tracey, another focus group participant from the African-Caribbean community in Liverpool, had described as a racially segregated city. She also noted the importance of highlighting the work of a black British writer through the 'Liverpool Reads'/*Small Island Read* programmes – a trenchant reminder that the most visible aspects of British arts and culture within the media and on the high street are still those produced by white elites:

> Martin said, you know, if we're talking about breaking down barriers and stuff, we need to tackle ignorance, um, and, and, you know, wild assumptions. And also, you know, let people – because I think that sometimes, people go out of the way to be racist, because of the hatred they've got in themselves. Sometimes people think – do it out of ignorance and if they had the information maybe, they'd think twice about it. You know, so, the – uh, I think [*Small Island*] is useful for breaking down barriers. And it's also great that a black author's been recognised at this level. You know, we've got the whole city – well, readers in the city – reading a book, um ... So I'm quite proud of Andrea really, she's done a good job.[24]

Kerry's commentary moves subtly between local and national realities to indicate the wide-scale structural transformations and shifts in cultural attitudes that need to occur in order to combat racism not just in her own city but also across the UK. Her pride in a British African-Caribbean woman whose work is being celebrated across the four city sites of *Small Island Read* also suggests an identification that operates beyond the scale of the local. For some Liverpool readers, then, the choice of a novel centred on London experiences is not a problem: the novel does not need to map directly on to their locale in order for them to produce analyses that connect up with their own knowledge and experience of 'race', class, and gender relations.

Like Kelly, other members of this focus group had a series of interesting and informed perspectives on interracial relations in Liverpool to bring to their interpretations of *Small Island*, and to the discussion of its suitability for the community-wide reading programme. Martin and Margaret (both Caucasian readers) have worked with asylum seekers and trade unionists, attempting to bring groups together to share first-hand stories in order to break through media stereotypes and people's internalized racism. Tracey's professional life as a social worker means that she has encountered various manifestations of racism, including physical violence. When prompted, various members of the group reflected on how far urban spaces in the city were 'classed' as well as 'raced'. Kelly noted, for example, 'It's like the city centre's in the middle, then you've got the north working-class, the south working-class, then you've got the middle-class in the, you know, going towards Crosby.'[25] Claire, a white woman in her early thirties, suggested that the south-side was more of 'a melting pot' than Kelly's initial analysis implied and she drew upon her knowledge of local history to underline her own lived experience of a racially mixed working-class neighbourhood:

> people seem to accept each other. Of course there's problems and [it] wasn't always peaceful, but it was almost like living in the 1950s, again with that attitude as well, the, the proper old, decent working-class kids out on the street, everybody takes care of each other. ... You've got generations ... of black people – and not just black people, Chinese, Liverpool's the oldest Chinese community in Europe as well. So in, in terms of that, the south end was, was where people, um, kind of settled as well. Sort of through the ports system, they came through the sea ... so I suppose it's, it's much more used to seeing different cultures as well over the, uh, you know the hundreds of years.[26]

These commentaries underline the fact that most people in this group were already deeply engaged with issues of difference before they read Levy's novel.

In common with the (white) women's reading group from Liverpool (quoted earlier) who initially foregrounded class values before 'race' relations in their consideration of Hortense's experiences, these focus group members suggest that *Small Island* can be read 'locally'. For some of the Liverpudlian readers, the lens of class provides a point of entry into the text's representation of racial difference while, for others, class relations are recognized as important co-vectors with 'race' (for example, Tracy's and Claire's comments). These approaches indicate how local knowledge about the intersection of class and 'race' within the city of Liverpool, while it is differently inflected by an individual's own experience and community identifications, can produce a 'local' reading of an apparently non-local story.

It is important to recognize, then, that readers engaged with *Small Island* at different levels, in different ways, and to different ends. As Elizabeth Long has noted within the context of North American book groups:

> Literature does have the power to allow some white readers a quasi-experiential expansion of empathy or identification across the racial divide, but it is a fragile power, for it rests on the reader's desire and ability to make an intersubjective bridge as she reads.[27]

Thus, the type of site which the novel affords for an examination of racist attitudes and structures is, like Gilroy's sense of lived multiculture, contingent on a number of factors, including a reader's own life experiences. Even when white readers make the 'intersubjective bridge' with Hortense and Gilbert by, for example, relating poverty and class-oppression during the 1940s and 1950s to racism, or by reflecting on the parallels between gender and 'race' inequities, the identification may be brief and does not necessarily lead to the development of more liberal views about racial difference. On the contrary, in some instances, unsettling thoughts about difference are 'made safe' by relocating them within the mid-twentieth-century time-frame and social context of Levy's novel. As one reader put it in the Chepstow group's discussion: 'Well I mean men went out to work and women did the cooking you know that's how it was.'[28]

Other readers reported ways in which the act of reading and sharing Levy's novel had been a 'learning' experience capable of transforming the reader's internalized assumptions. Susan, a white focus group participant in Liverpool, had lent the novel to her mother because she was concerned that, as they grow older, her parents have 'got a bit more prejudiced and bigoted'. Susan's other motive – 'to [get] her off Dick Francis at last' – suggests her understanding of a literary hierarchy within which Levy's novel ranks higher than genre fiction and is thus (implicitly) not only better writing, but 'better' for the reader in a moral or educational sense:

> It really hit home to my mum that then when [Gilbert] came to this country and was treated as though he wasn't w – yeah he was, you know, uh, discriminated against – um and, and he thought that he was coming home to the motherland in a way to a, a t – a country that would really look after him. That's what struck home to my mum and she talked about that a lot on the phone to me, and that's why she gave the book to her friends, because she, she couldn't believe that bit. It, it was, it was, um, it was an education to her in a way. And she was very shocked about the whole education system that was exported out to the colonies. And I think that's why it – if it makes – you know, if it's made one person sit up and actually address, you know, an innate prejudice, or you know, 'People come here to take our jobs', that sort of thing, I think it's, it's been valuable.[29]

As she describes her mother's response to *Small Island*, Susan also articulates another way in which the novel can be connective when the experience of reading is shared, bridging intergenerational difference. During our research we heard about other kinds of 'connection' around, and through, the discussion and reading of *Small Island*, including the sharing of painful personal stories of poverty and sexism. Within the Liverpool group, where trust has been established among members, it becomes safe for two women to talk about painful memories because they have been prompted by incidents in the novel. The respectful turn-taking within this group and the 'I hear what you're saying' type of comments which members offered in response to personal stories, demonstrate how, within a book group context, the reading of fiction that explores under-represented experiences and aspects of history can enable the validation of other types of silenced histories within readers' own lives. Differences of class and economic circumstances among group members become articulated and understood through storytelling. Thus, in some cases, Levy's text offers a meeting-place within which readers can elaborate their own subjectivity alongside or even against the grain of the characters represented in the novel.

As our analysis in the second part of this essay suggests, actual readers of Levy's novel use their discussions of the book to establish various types of connection or 'meeting'. These range from the material, face-to-face encounters of the book group itself, to ephemeral moments of inter-generational or cross-cultural connection. For some readers, sharing and re-reading *Small Island* with others enables a critical examination of British imperialism and its contemporary legacies. This appears to be the type of cross-cultural and multicultural work that the sponsors and organizers of *Small Island Read* hoped that the mass-read would perform. However, the dialogic and reflexive processes which lead readers to produce these instances of critique accord more with Gilroy's notion of 'multiculture' as a series of eruptions that occur only to dissipate within everyday life. The provisionality of 'multiculture' and its vernacular formation is mirrored, or rather refracted, in the fleeting and sometimes ambiguous nature of the instances within which readers recognize the textual 'Other', or make connections between institutionally reinforced inequities of gender and 'race'. Rather than producing the 'social glue' that reconnects the citizens of divided cities, then, the mass-read of *Small Island* creates something more akin to fragile threads among those who choose to participate.

Nevertheless, reading *Small Island* together, a project facilitated by the *Small Island Read 2007* programme, offers the potential for meeting-places to be imagined and even actualized. Jenny Hartley has noted that book groups offer 'a forum for a level of debate and conversation not easily found elsewhere' in contemporary society, even if the outcomes of these conversations cannot be guaranteed.[30] In this context, we remain caught between the opening epigraphs of our essay. If *Small Island*, mobilized as it was by the mass-read event, potentially fosters linkages and connections across cultures, it does not *necessarily* serve as a bridge, crossover or meeting-point between them.

NOTES

1. 'Beyond the Book' participant focus group (3) Liverpool, 19 February 2007. In this essay, quotations are taken from interview transcripts. Verbatim transcription practices have been followed by both research teams. However, 'Beyond the Book' received permission to use the first and, in some cases, family names of research participants, while 'Devolving Diasporas' have designated speakers S1, S2, etc., except where it became impossible to assign speech to a particular speaker, hence S★ is employed. For reasons of confidentiality and data protection, none of these transcripts is in the public domain.

2. 'Beyond the Book' interview with Beccy Jones, Bluecoat Arts Centre, Liverpool, 21 February 2007.

3. Both of these projects investigate, with different emphases, contemporary cultures of reading, locally and globally. 'Beyond the Book' is a collaborative project investigating mass-reading events in the UK, USA, and Canada, which was funded by the AHRC 2005-8. A multi-disciplinary team employed mixed methods, including on-line surveys, focus groups with readers, interviews with event organizers, and participation-observation of events in order to investigate shared reading as a social practice and to examine the power relations among the various agents involved in selected community-, region- and nation-wide reading events.
   See <http://www.beyondthebookproject.org> 'Devolving Diasporas' is a three-year AHRC funded project exploring the relationship between reading, migration, and location by recording and analysing book group discussions across the UK and in specific locations in India, Canada, the Caribbean, and Africa.
   See <http://www.devolvingdiasporas.com/>

4. Statistics and demographics cited by Liverpool City Council at:
   <http://www.liverpool.gov.uk/News/Facts_and_figures/index.asp> accessed 22 April 2009.

5. James Procter, *Writing Black Britain 1948-1998* (Manchester: Manchester UP, 2000), p. 3.

6. 'The Reader' organization acts as an umbrella for several reading-centred projects, including 'Liverpool Reads' and the award-winning 'Get Into Reading' programme which has worked with more than 80 groups of people in the Wirral and Liverpool to date. These groups include recovering addicts, young LGBT people, seniors, people with mental health challenges, new immigrants and asylum seekers.
   For 'The Reader', see: <http://thereader.org.uk/>
   For 'Get Into Reading', see: <http://reachingout.thereader.org.uk/>.

7. See, for example, Bea Colley, the 'Liverpool Reads' co-ordinator cited in 'Movie Writer Leads Book Campaign', 25 September 2005 at <http://news.bbc.co.uk/1/hi/england/merseyside/4280592.stm> accessed 23 April 2009.

8. For a critical analysis of how British publishers constructed the contemporary genre of the 'crossover book', see Claire Squires, *Marketing Literature: The Making of Contemporary Writing in Britain* (London: Palgrave Macmillan, 2007), pp.147-75.

9. To maintain the connection with schools and children in the city, 'Liverpool Reads' promoted two texts for younger readers alongside *Small Island*: Benjamin Zephaniah's

Refugee Boy (London: Bloomsbury, 2001) and Mary Hoffman's *Amazing Grace* (London: Frances Lincoln, 1991). Both books deal with issues of racism and/or the experiences of immigrants and asylum seekers in the UK, although in different historical periods from Levy's novel. All three books were adopted by the four cities in the *Small Island Read* project but the selections for younger readers were more heavily promoted by 'Liverpool Reads' on their website, and through many events aimed at young people and school children.

10. See, for example, Elizabeth Long, *Book Clubs: Women and the Uses of Reading in Everyday Life* (Chicago: Chicago UP, 2003); Elizabeth McHenry, *Forgotten Readers: Recovering the Lost History of African American Literary Societies* (Durham, NC: Duke UP, 2002), Heather Murray, *Come, Bright Improvement: The Literary Societies of Nineteenth-Century Ontario* (Toronto: U of Toronto P, 2002).

11. See, for example, DeNel Rehberg Sedo, 'Readers in Reading Groups: An On-Line Survey of Face-to-Face And Virtual Book Clubs', *Convergence*, 1:9 (2003) 66-90.

12. See, for example, Long's discussion of the 'color line' in reading groups, *Book Clubs,* p. xv.

13. *Small Island Read* was planned to coincide with the Abolition of the Slave Trade bicentennial in 2007.

14. Melanie Kelly, 'Small Island Read 2007': Evaluation Report, p. 2. <http://www.smallislandread.com/default.asp> accessed 09.10.07.

15. Melanie Kelly, p. 7. The event was sponsored primarily by Arts Council England and the Heritage Lottery Fund.

16. Photographs can be found on various pages at: <http://www.bristolreads.com/small_island_read/index.html>

17. As Mette Hjort defines it 'corporate multiculturalism is motivated, not by notions of dignity or worth, but by a set of economic concerns. A certain form of multicultural literacy – the ability to speak a foreign tongue and to grasp the self-understandings of members of certain groups – may be sought for purely self-interested reasons'. In Adam Muller, ed., *Concepts of Culture* (Calgary: U of Calgary P, 2005), p. 137

18. Paul Gilroy, *After Empire: Multiculture or Postcolonial Melancholia* (London: Routledge, 2004).

19. 'Beyond the Book' participant focus group (5), Liverpool, 21 February 2007.

20. Long, *Book Clubs,* p. 176.

21. 'Devolving Diasporas' reading group, Liverpool, 8 May 2007.

22. While Liverpool, Hull, Glasgow and Bristol were the hubs for *Small Island Read 2007,* the event radiated outwards to include areas of South West England (e.g. Penzance) and Wales (e.g. Chepstow).

23. 'Devolving Diasporas' reading group, Chepstow, 6 June 2007.

24. 'Beyond the Book' participant and non-participant focus group (6), 22 February 2007.

25. Ibid.

26. Ibid.

27. Long, *Book Clubs,* p. 186.

28. 'Devolving Diasporas' reading group, Chepstow, 6 June 2007.

29. 'Beyond the Book' participant focus group (2), 17 February 2007.

30. Jenny Hartley, *Reading Groups* (Oxford: Oxford UP, 2001), p. 42.

SHAMSHAD KHAN

Manchester Snow

I. street by street
can I get into your dreams
the way you get into mine?

a see-through glass ball
filled with a handful of water and glitter

I shake the ball in the future
will I dream you or will you dream me?

I get to know myself better
every time you answer

and every time my mind goes blank

Manchester everything I love about you now
I loved about you then

fake gothic promises
straight talking red bricks

choose me they said choose me
and I did

you were honest
openly pretending to be what you weren't

not as big as London
you mocked me

close enough to Leeds
let's see if a rose can change colour

if she comes
let's see if she can leave

II. graffiti

I cannot take my eyes off you
I cannot look directly at you

pavement slabs
flooded gutters

my mind falls
my heart writes

so I can see what I am saying
or what you are trying to tell me

over new bridges
beside dark water

in the shade of Victorian buildings
I catch the 192

Romanian, Irish, Iranian, African Mancunians
slip sliding condensation and conversations

on the top deck
youngsters rearranging the English language

messages on the roofs of bus shelters
a bottle, a boot, a dandelion shoot

on an ordinary street
something is looking for you

III. the city's quiz

Like all the others
what I thought I came for

and what I end up doing here
don't exactly match

once you've redirected me
you start questioning my motives

the poet's purpose in a city?

I don't know the answer so I point

keep pointing you say
go there and stay there until you are given a reason to move

I've wandered from landmark to landmark
proudly pointing visitors to their destinations

stumbling across old haunts
I point at the ghost of my self

why a poet?

you ask me seemingly simple questions
that I find impossible to answer

I try pointing
you don't bat an eyelid

your most valued experience as a poet?

I remember a very long night
all daylight and ink

why did you come here?

you chuckle at my silence
and point to the door

IV. calling you home

I have recited poetry between
the explosions of fireworks

had my words swept away
from the microphone by the wind

performing in a different place
being heard by strangers' ears

I am more playful
I don't act quite myself

I break habits
realizing how much of being is pretending

when I am away from you
I talk about you

people see you in me
I like what they see

I miss you
I write about you

when I get back
come on I say

let's change some of these old routines
it can be fun

pretending to be real

V. getting tagged
what you read to me when my eyes were falling closed
what we read in unison

what I took down from low shelves
what I reached for

what you read by heart
what I unintentionally overheard

in everything that reached my ears
I heard you

like a book I can read from when you are not there
I read at my pace

your silent voice
spray painted on my internal wall

VI. rapid eye movements
you dreamed of me
when I was walking the streets of Leeds

I heard your name but other than that
you hardly existed for me

I can't imagine myself
not having met you

you have shaped my relationship
with glitter filled skies

you have made me accept
the people who left us

in your grey streets
I found my home
what I did not notice when we met
is a familiar inconvenience now

grains of pollution
crystallizing into six-sided perfections

a damp hat that will not let me forget
why it rains

VII. another loft conversion

Manchester where do you see yourself in twenty years?

don't answer straightaway

let your mind drop into my heart
let blood mix with light

answer after you've decided
that you'll stay

Contemporary British Poetry and the Transcultural Imagination

RENUKA RAJARATNAM

> Without my map, will I be the same person?
> Will I know where I am, where I have been?[1]
>
> I move in many cultures, my friend –
> Of necessity I make them my own.[2]
>
> Somali refugee in Jamaican domain
> Bangla boy in a Pakistani terrain
> Vietnamese in poor white district
> They know they have to take their chances.[3]

The epigraphs above indicate the broad discursive parameters of the following discussion, which foregrounds the contradictions, ambivalences, and collisions that proliferate in contemporary British poetry. The central aims of this essay are: to trace the resourceful evolution of transcultural models that have been harnessed by the hybrid aesthetics of Britain's diverse globalized localities; and to explore how hybrid poetic subjectivities are placed within the global collective, given that they move beyond localism towards a transcultural vision, a vision that claims the right to global citizenship.

Contemporary Britain is uniquely positioned as a nation of devolved cultures where notions of homogeneity and authenticity have largely been replaced by a sense of cultural hybridity that admits a new version of cosmopolitanism.[4] I wish to demonstrate how poetry participates in, and responds to, these hybrid formulations. Focusing on the work of Jackie Kay (Glasgow/Manchester), Debjani Chatterjee (Sheffield), Patience Agbabi (London) and Shamshad Khan (Manchester), my essay examines how Britain's glocalities creatively collide, merge, and transform into worlds of contingency, contradiction, and multiplicity.

The notion of transculturalism emerges in relation to the concepts of multiculturalism and cosmopolitanism. Its main critical and creative shortcomings lie in its utopian vision. Nevertheless, the transcultural imagination is emerging as a significant feature of twenty-first century literature as it finds affinities with the contemporary discourses of postmodernism, postcolonialism, and post-ethnicity.[5] Forging new affiliations as well with the cosmopolitan ethics of tolerance on the one hand and the promotion of the 'ethics of co-existence' on the other, transculturalism engages with postmodernism's relentless dismantling of identity and stability.[6] It is also necessary to theorize the transcultural aesthetic in relation to post-ethnicity as the fundamental principle of both creative models. The transcultural aesthetic seeks to transcend roots in order to find liberating spaces in an imaginary elsewhere. While there seems to be a difficulty in locating the precise origins and the evolution of transculturalism, it is yet more difficult to locate artists creatively or to classify their influences. The poetry I am about to discuss reflects a range of attempts by poets whose work offers a transcultural vision to find creative emancipation *within* mobility rather than stationing it in particular sites of culture. By responding to the new economic and socio-cultural patterns of Britain's glocalized contexts, many poets who draw on the transcultural imagination also set out to challenge traditional critical constructs of how poetry is read or written.

In the discussion that follows, I identify three core aspects of transculturalism: the contradictory nature of difference, multiplicity within movement, and the hybrid poetics of cosmopolitanism. Contradiction, multiplicity, and hybridity, then, are at the core of transcultural poetic configurations, though with varied features, each entailing their own complexity. Jackie Kay's poetry explores the inherent contradictions contained within the cultural paradigm of multiple difference, and in ways that expose the limitations of the existing cultural paradigm. The Yorkshires and Indias of Debjani Chatterjee's work, meanwhile, are infused with the global in ways that reflect the contemporary movement of travelling cultures. Finally, I examine the way in which the performance poetry of Patience Agbabi and Shamshad Khan explores the hybrid poetics of cosmopolitanism.[7]

In order to understand the evolution of Jackie Kay's[8] hybrid poetic configurations, it is important to take into account her flexible creative sensibility, which resourcefully mixes and merges diverse genres, styles, and cultural dialects. This section will examine the political agency that propels this creative sensibility. Above all, Kay is exceedingly alert to exclusivist definitions of cultural identity. Through the twin tropes of her poetic oeuvre, which are essentially adoption and adaptation, Kay constantly confronts and challenges the divisive constructs often to be found in conventional poetry bound by elitist ties, and rewrites the political and cultural contours of particular g/localities.

In an early poem entitled 'Kail and Callaloo', the speaker is vexed by the inquiry into her 'origins' by officials who are dealing with passport and job applications. The officials' belief as to the impossibility of her multiple identifications exposes the limitations of conventional conceptions of identity: 'Celtic – Afro – Caribbean /in answer to the origin question; /they think that's a contradiction. /how kin ye be both?'[9] The speaker's implicit response to the question of origin emphasizes the authenticity of her own 'Scottishness', which is able to reproduce faithfully the local Glaswegian accent from her own intimate knowledge of its cadences. In this way, she establishes herself as a cultural 'insider'. What is at stake here is the credibility of this perceived contradiction, which is undermined by her continual shape-shifting. The poem confronts a nationalist politics and offers, in the words of Matthew Brown, 'the next generation … a notion of identity and citizenship predicated on a cosmopolitan merger of local and transnational spaces'.[10] The poem mobilizes a transcultural perspective in order to recast Scotland as a globalized locality.

Kay's work from *The Adoption Papers* to *Life Mask* (2005) and the recent collection, *Darling,* has been both progressive and regressive (atavistic, in the Jungian sense). The potential ambivalence lies in the necessity to trace her roots on one hand, and yet transcend them on the other. The acclaimed poem, 'Pride', from the 1998 collection *Off Colour*, explores the quest for a sense of certainty in originating from, and belonging to, a specific locale. The speaker of the poem befriends a stranger, an African man, on the train to Glasgow. He instinctively recognizes her Nigerian Ibo origins and invites her to identify herself as Nigerian:

> My whole face changed into a map,
> and the stranger on the train
> located even the name
> of my village in Nigeria.[11]

The poem indulges in a dramatic fantasy of return, in which the persona celebrates arriving on the 'hot dust, the red road' of her native land where 'her feet/start … to dance'.[12] The dream of belonging is reflected in the envy she expresses for the Nigerian man, who seems so certain of his origin, home, and heritage. His sense of pride comes from an essential feeling of belonging, which presents a striking contrast to the speaker's contradictory positioning: 'His face had a look, /… the most startling thing, pride/ a quality of being certain'.[13] However, since it is impossible to tell whether the man on the train is real or not – hence the fantasy of return

– the poem's chief anxiety lies in the unattainability of a pride based on a form of belonging that is potentially an illusion. In *Life Mask*, meanwhile, Kay depicts an autobiographical journey to Nigeria to meet her birth father. The poem, 'Things Fall Apart', is a poignant exploration of human relationship and its tragic losses: 'I could see his eyes behind the hard alabaster./A father, no more real, still less real.'[14] Here, Kay's desire to reunite with her biological father and perhaps attain a sense of certainty turns out to be a failed endeavour. Her father tells her that she was his 'past sin'.[15] Taken together, then, 'Pride' and 'Things Fall Apart' dramatize the tension between the desire to belong on the one hand, and, on the other, recognition of the elusive nature of such a quest.

The transformative process of identity and its consequent splintering is a recurrent theme in Kay's poetry. In 'My face is a map' from the collection *Darling*, Kay describes the uncanny connection between a person's face and a geographical location. She deftly uses global metamorphosis as a creative trope to foreground the crisis of confounding geography as well as individual identity. Closely resembling Elizabeth Bishop's poem, 'The Map', which grapples with similar issues, Kay's persona attempts to overcome her facial impairment by accepting her legacy of contradictions although it has severely distorted her self-image: 'Without my map, will I be the same person?/ Will I know where I am; where I have been?'[16]

If Kay's poetry undermines the rhetoric of national identity and belonging, the work of Delhi-born Debjani Chatterjee adopts the alternative approach of exploring a hybrid identity that has been formulated by the experience of 'travelling cultures'.[17] Chatterjee's migratory subjectivity explores the liminal routes of travel to multiple places, including India, Japan, Bangladesh, Hong Kong, Egypt and Britain. Cited alongside the other epigraphs to this essay, Chatterjee's lines, 'I move in many cultures, my friend – /Of necessity I make them my own',[18] indicate her notion of multiplicity as a generative experience entailing the manifold openings of new meanings. In a glocality where differences co-exist as well as collide, what does it mean to make a culture your own? Does ownership mobilize a form of political agency that seeks a cultural coalition or a compromise? Or is the poet merely indulging in the rhetoric of global integration? Whatever the point of view, Chatterjee's lines provoke questions that probe fundamental negotiations of identity in the diaspora, questions that reflect crucial tensions between cultural assimilation, transformation, and translation.

'To the English Language' addresses the hegemonic power of the language and its long association with colonialism. Confessing that she 'learnt to love the language the hard way',[19] the speaker reveals the effort required to combat the intimidating nature of this heritage. Mustering strength from her movement between many worlds and their languages,[20] she confronts the hierarchies embodied in the English language:

> I do not come to your rhythms empty-handed
> – the treasures of other traditions are mine
> so many Koh-i-noors, to be claimed.[21]

Here, English is presented as a 'Koh-i-noor', the Indian diamond owned originally by the Mughal royalty and now a British crown jewel. The diamond's triple heritage serves as a reminder that languages are formed and enriched by multiple influences, a legacy that gives her some ownership of it. Above all, the speaker's hybrid subjectivity is multivocal: 'I speak in many tongues, my friend – /Moulded by the black experience./Languages are my inheritance.'[22] Here, the speaker's creative agency is imbued with a polemic that destabilizes nationalist notions of monoculturalism by suggesting that the English language is manifestly the consequence of previous dialogues between and across cultures. It is this impulse that animates transcultural creativity. Chatterjee's transcultural imagination appeals to what Homi K. Bhabha describes as the 'ethics of co-existence', emerging from a 'social space which has to be continually shared with others, and from which solidarity is not simply based on similarity but on the recognition of difference'.[23] This is a pertinent observation to the poetry of both Kay and Chatterjee, predicated as it is on an ethical right to shared existence in a society where identity is necessarily multiple, an inevitable consequence of global movement brought about by migration, war, exile and travel in recent times.

Collective expression has been a much foregrounded feature of postcolonial social formations. While there have been considerable changes in the themes and emphases of postcolonial writing since the 1980s, the 'collective telling'[24] of Chatterjee's poetry places her work in direct correspondence with the work of writers, such as Imtiaz Dharker and Grace Nichols, in whose writing the politics of selfhood was deeply engaged with wider social concerns. Chatterjee's 'The Arrival', from her collection *Namaskar: New and Selected Poems*, is congruent with this tradition, since it frames the experience of exile in collective terms:

> The cardinal winds have brought us here.
> Now battered, now buoyant, we survived.
> What mattered most was getting it clear:
> No longer strangers, we have arrived.[25]

The poem foregrounds the solidarity of South Asian communities who resist being intimidated by foreignness and assert their belonging by means of the fundamental act of their 'arrival' on strange shores. It is the collective manner in which the arrival is announced that empowers an assertion of belonging. Neither, for Chatterjee, is such collective assertion without substance. Based in Sheffield, Chatterjee has contributed to a diverse range of work, including the steel industry, education, hospitals and community building. Furthermore, she co-directs Sahitya Press, which promotes Asian-British and multilingual writing (the history of which is recounted by Chatterjee herself in this issue of *Moving Worlds*). Conceiving of a responsible world citizenship as based on the paradox that "there are no others ... there are *many* cultural others',[26] contemporary g/localism advocates a viable transcultural-communal future. Within this transcultural context, notions of what constitutes 'Asianness' or 'Britishness' are highly contestable, as Chatterjee asserts:

I am more than I wear: Asian British ...
Sari or jeans, I am the daughter
of Birmingham and Southall.[27]

The changing patterns of g/local affiliation have formulated a cosmopolitan social site which proves to be extremely beneficial for younger poets, many of whom place their individual experiences within this resourceful creative arena. Each poet makes her own transcultural forays into the collective, teasing out new meanings in poetry through a blend of performance, music, and various dramatic elements. The remaining section of this essay considers how poetry can signify differently according to variations in public presentation and performance by focusing on the work of Patience Agbabi and Shamshad Khan.

My aim is to foreground the poetry of Agbabi and Khan as 'British voices'. They are poets who insist on distinguishing their voices from the preceding 'postcolonial' generations by naming their Britishness as a first principle. Much of their work is informed by their staying power in the cosmopolitan cities and their negotiations with the social space through a poetic articulation of inclusive citizenship. Since their cultural affiliations are particularly complex, I wish to demonstrate how, as poets, their subjectivities and identities are hybridized in ways that have brought about a new aesthetic. In my interviews with Agbabi and Khan, which were conducted in Chennai (India) and Manchester (UK) in 2007 and 2008, both poets declared that 'performance' was only a subordinate characteristic to the 'actual work with words'.[28] They claimed that the theatrical elements were mainly used to enhance communal involvement and affirmed their roles as poets and not mere performers.[29]

Born in London, 1965, Patience Agbabi has published three volumes of poetry: *R.A.W* (1995), *Tranformatrix* (2000), and *Bloodshot Monochrome* (2008). Although she is of Nigerian descent, Agbabi claims the place was not much of an inspiration for her. She shares some aspects of Jackie Kay's biography, having been adopted by white parents and self-consciously positive of her mixed cultural identity. Claiming that hers is 'a very British voice', Agbabi asserts that it is a voice that has evolved from within the British tradition and she is 'a part of this tradition'.[30] As a poet, Agbabi celebrates a transcultural space of imagination, which she finds to be creatively liberating and, in my opinion, her work for this reason vividly captures the power of her lived experience in London. Agbabi describes the city's cosmopolitanism through a fusion of poetry and music that reflect the mood, momentum, and energy of urban life. Her stylized blurring of the boundaries between reality and fantasy is strikingly innovative. Through a skilful manipulation of the techniques of surrealism, her poetry metamorphoses everyday environments into extraordinary ones, transforming them into absurd scenarios of estrangement. 'UFO Woman (pronounced as OOFOE)' from her collection *Transformatrix* depicts an African Caribbean woman as a cosmopolitan product of the metropolis. The speaker of the poem is an ordinary black woman who is wittily transformed into an alien who has stepped off a spaceship:

> I've learnt the language. … Mother Earth
> do you *read* me? When they stamp my passport
> ALIEN at Heath Row? Did I come third
> in the World Race?[31]

Aimed at a society driven by intolerance in the face of cultural difference, Agbabi's poem adopts a cavalier tone to address a serious issue. As her 'weirdo' persona meanders through the streets of London, she is met with unfriendly 'kids with crystal/cut ice-cream cones and tin-can eyes' asking, 'Why/don't UFO back to your own planet?'[32] The poem in six-line stanzas is tightly structured, and is imbued with the power of storytelling, satire, humour and critique. In the last stanza, the UFO woman prepares for 'lift off', 'playing *Revelations* /and my intergalactic mobile ON,/ call me, I'll be surfing the galaxy/searching for that perfect destination',[33] a utopian elsewhere, a transcultural glocality.

Apart from her impressive handling of a wide range of poetic forms, ranging from monologues to sonnets and sestinas, Agbabi's poems are wonderfully rendered in terms of feeling and idea. Her splendid evocation of urban funk music, which describes a state of mind as drug-induced and fraught with chaos on the one hand and a sharp logical sense of order on the other, is portrayed with humour in 'Ajax': 'Fly the Tube. I'd rather take a plane/Concorde, to be exact, high on cocaine'.[34] London's fragmentation and its 'split personality' is described in relation to a high-octane world of drugs and disco.

Agbabi's experimental aesthetic culminates in her recent collection, *Bloodshot Monochrome* (2008). The collection is organized into monologues and multi-vocal sequences. Where *Transformatrix,* as Agbabi notes in an interview, was inspired by 'musicality (particularly … rap, ska and the blues) as a technique of delivery',[35] *Bloodshot Monochrome* is an exuberant celebration of hybrid poetic form. In an inventive sequence of sonnets called 'The Problem Pages', the speaker enters into dialogue with 'dead' poets, from John Milton to June Jordan. Within the contemporary 'question and answer' format, conflict is presented in the form of a question, while the solution follows in the form of an answer provided by 'Patience'. This format facilitates a dialogue between contemporary and traditional voices. A poem in this sequence, 'Joy and Woe', is narrated by the early Elizabethan poet, Henry Howard, Earl of Surrey, and the issue of hybrid creativity is shown to have been a matter of concern even when Henry Howard crafted his English Renaissance sonnets:

> *Dear Patience,* I'm the Mont Blanc of blank,
> verse, the Renoir of rhyme. I've invented a
> hybrid sonnet that retains the Italian elegance
> yet is more suited to the modern English
> tongue …
>
> Craft your discipline on the page and the stage.
> Reinvent yourself. [36]

In this subversive interplay of past and present voices, Elizabethan and contemporary, Agbabi playfully unfolds how the processes of poetic practice are often fuelled by intercultural strategies.

Born in Leeds, Shamshad Khan presently lives and works in Manchester. Her poetry, which has been broadcast on BBC Radio 3 and 4, is theatrical and multilingual with strong musical and visual elements. Whereas Debjani Chatterjee's work conveys an ideal of reconciling cultural or political difference, Khan's work is far more guarded in its approach to British cosmopolitanism:

We're all black
brothers
when there's plenty.
but when things are short
a Jew is a Jew
Black means African not Asian
and Asian doesn't mean Chinese.[37]

Indeed, a similar context is evoked in the third epigraph to this essay, and Khan's poetry repeatedly discusses the pressures that scarcity of material resources brings to bear on interracial solidarities. Khan teases out the fragility of British multiculturalism in times of sudden political or economic crisis.

Khan's debut collection, *Megalomaniac*, has a unique dramatic quality that subverts conventional wisdom about the need to subjugate the ego. In the title poem of her collection, she berates the 'classical conditioning' received through the formal education system:

telling you what to do where and when
the bell
period 4 science block biology
conditioned reflexes.[38]

Elsewhere in the poem, she scorns institutionalized religion as yet another mind-controlling mechanism that places constraints on creativity and freedom:

I put my scarf on
round the corner from the mosque
there's lots of rules
don't do that
do that like this.[39]

Instead the poem celebrates the freedom of the ego from the fetters of institutional entrapment. The ego seeks apolitical spaces beyond the ideologically-bounded categories of race, gender, and sexuality. In embracing the ego, she taps into the power of desire: 'I become the object of all my desires / I become the thing that I want.'[40] However, this power is also shown to be illusory. By deploying dexterous postmodern stylistics, Khan engages in self-reflexive play by reinscribing identity and desire within a condition of 'simulacra', a term deployed by Baudrillard to signify 'replicas that substitute for a vanishing real'.[41] Khan's illusion of megalomania is both real and 'vanishing'. In this sense, it closely resembles 'maya', or illusion, whereby the unreal world of appearances constitutes the only visible and tangible manifestation of a reality that often eludes sensory knowing. Locating the poem's insight within oscillating realities and illusions, then, Khan observes that globalized localities are fraught with contradiction:

> Somali refugees in Jamaican domain
> Bangla boy in Pakistani terrain …
> then some no hoper reaches for a gun
> because he reckons he's never gonna get what he wanted.[42]

These lines are emblematic of the extent to which multiracial localities figure in her work as ambivalent social spaces that are riven with conflicting allegiances. More importantly, they alert us to the precarious nature of multiple formations, which are fraught with contradictions, owing to the inconsistent nature of difference and diversity, and are prone to both affiliation as well as dispersal. This poetic consciousness is reflected in the experimental nature of her verse. Her poems, it must also be remembered, are delivered in a range of social environments and the performance varies immensely to fit the audience and occasion. In the flexible responsiveness of her poetic performances to the specificities and contingencies of the contexts in which they take place, Khan's poetry similarly presents British civic spaces as subject to constant revision.

As Khan's poetry makes clear, Britain's globalized localities are often riven with conflict, that derives from the need, especially where material resources are under strain, to negotiate obsolete perceptions of cultural identity, nationhood, and belonging. Nevertheless, the transcultural poetics that have emerged from various locations within Glasgow, Manchester, Leeds and London reflect the exciting if often bewildering 'g/local' interactivity of the social formations to be found. The poetry of Kay, Chatterjee, Agbabi and Khan articulates a confident self-declaration of inclusive cultural citizenship which is persistently threatened by racism. By prominently foregrounding the ambivalent experience of being located at one and the same time within and without Britain, these poets imaginatively transform 'stable locations'[43] into mobile worlds re-scripted with new meanings and new possibilities. In the process, the poetic metamorphosis, which is strongly motivated by a cosmopolitan world view, challenges the readers to conceive of an identity that is not only locally situated or nationally bound but is also shaped by a global belonging.

NOTES

1. Jackie Kay, *Darling: New and Selected Poems* (Tarset: Bloodaxe Books, 2007).
2. Debjani Chatterjee, *I was that woman* (Frome: Hippopotamus Press, 1989).
3. Shamshad Khan, *Megalomaniac* (Cambridge: Salt Publishing, 2007).
4. Ulrich Beck, *The Cosmopolitan Vision*, trans., Ciaran Cronin (Cambridge: Polity Press, 2006).
5. Post-ethnicity finds its affinities with transculturalism by seeking an appreciation for different communities of descent and thereby potentially providing ample space for new communities to flourish. Globalized localities hold post-ethnic potential promoting 'solidarity of wide scope that includes people with different ethnic and racial background'. David Hollinger, *Postethnic America: Beyond Multiculturalism* (New York: Basic Books, 1995), pp. 3-4.
6. As propounded by cultural theorist, Homi K. Bhabha, in *The Location of Culture* (London: Routledge, 1994), p. 38.
7. 'Hybrid poetics of cosmopolitanism' in my view explores the imaginative process of lived and transformed experiences of metropolitan life characterized by the proliferation of multiple cultures.
8. Jackie Kay, born in 1961 to a Scottish mother and Nigerian father, was adopted by a white Scottish couple at birth. She grew up in Glasgow, a city which evokes the sense of the poet 'being outside with being inside Scotland' (Matthew Brown, p. 221, see fn 10). At present, she lives in Manchester and teaches at Newcastle University. Kay's career began as a dramatist in 1986 with the staging of her first play, *Chiaroscuro*, followed by *Twice Over*, 1988. She burst into the world of poetry in 1991 with the publication of her acclaimed collection, *The Adoption Papers*. Currently with eight volumes to her credit, Kay has also published a novel, and short stories, and has collaborated with the media to produce films on poetry.
9. Jackie Kay, 'Kail and Callaloo', in *Charting the Journey: Writings by Black and Third World Women*, eds. Shabnam Grewal et al (London: Sheba Feminist Publishers, 1988), p. 195.
10. Matthew Brown, 'In / outside Scotland: Race and Citizenship in the work of Jackie Kay', in *The Edinburgh Companion to Contemporary Scottish Literature*, ed., Berthold Schoene (Edinburgh: Edinburgh UP, 2007), pp. 219-25.
11. Jackie Kay, *Off Colour* (Newcastle upon Tyne: Bloodaxe Books, 1998), pp. 62-63.
12. Kay, *Off Colour*, p. 63.
13. Kay, *Off Colour*, p. 63.
14. Jackie Kay, *Life Mask* (Tarset: Bloodaxe Books, 2005), p. 33.
15. Kay, *Life Mask*, p. 33.
16. Kay, *Life Mask*, p. 33.
17. See James Clifford, *Routes: Travel and Translation in the late Twentieth Century* (Cambridge, MA: Harvard UP, 1997).
18. Chatterjee, *I was that woman*, p. 34.
19. Chatterjee, *I was that woman*, p. 34.
20. Chatterjee, *I was that woman*, p. 34.
21. Debjani Chatterjee, *Namaskar: New and Selected Poems* (Bradford: Redbeck Press, 2004), p. 28.
22. Chatterjee, *I was that woman*, p. 34.
23. Bhabha, *The Location of Culture*, p. 38.
24. The notion of collective experience stems from Deleuze and Guattaris' view that almost everything involved in the black 'minor' literature is political, since there is no space for individual concerns to remain individual. Marginalized communities often intimidated by the dominant culture adopted collective expression in order to

foreground their solidarity. See Giles Deleuze and Felix Guattari, 'What is Minor Literature?' in *Kafka: Toward a Minor Literature* (Minneapolis: U of Minnesota P, 1986), p. 34.

25. Chatterjee, *Namaskar*, p. 56.

26. John Tomlinson, *Globalization and Culture* (Cambridge: Polity Press, 1999), p. 194.

27. Chatterjee, *Namaskar*, p.137.

28. Renuka Rajaratnam, 'Poetry Unplugged: In conversation with Patience Agbabi', *The Hindu, Sunday Magazine*, 2007, p. 3.

29. Lemn Sissay outlines this argument in his 'News from the Beat', *Poetry Review*, 96:4 (2006), 122-23.

30. Rajaratnam, 'Poetry Unplugged', p. 3.

31. Patience Agbabi, *Transformatrix* (Edinburgh: Canongate Books, 2000), pp. 15-17.

32. Agbabi, *Transformartrix*, p. 15.

33. Agbabi, *Transformatrix*, p. 17.

34. Agbabi, *Transformatrix*, p. 69.

35. Rajaratnam, 'Poetry Unplugged', p. 3.

36. Patience Agbabi, *Bloodshot Monochrome* (Edinburgh: Canongate Books, 2008), p. 33.

37. Shamshad Khan, *Megalomaniac* (Cambridge: Salt Publishing, 2007), p. 81.

38. Khan, *Megalomaniac*, p. 70.

39. Khan, *Megalomaniac*, p. 69.

40. Khan, *Megalomaniac*, p. 68.

41. Ian Gregson, *Postmodern Literature* (London: Arnold, 2004), pp. 5-7.

42. Khan, *Megalomaniac*, p. 68.

43. John McLeod, *Postcolonial London: Rewriting the Metropolis* (London: Routledge, 2004), pp. 7, 15.

The Dance

MULI AMAYE

Issy stood with her head bowed and waited. She could sense the shift in the audience as the tension stretched its way across the seats. There was a rustling at the side of the stage. The last drummer took his place. But she could only think about one thing as she stood in the thick stage air.

The first beat of the drum vibrated through the floor and up her slim legs to fill her chest. She turned her head to the left and the right and saw the pity in the other dancers' eyes. They were all thinking the same thing. She knew it. She knew that even as they pitied her, they were relieved it wasn't happening to them. They belonged.

Each time she lifted her head she had to close her eyes as the lights glared deep into them. She wasn't standing in a good place. She wondered if this is how the sun would be when she got off the plane. Would she stand there blinded before hands pulled her away and maybe even handcuffed her? Thumping the rhythm on the boards, she circled with the others. Today she was free. But tomorrow.

They'd been practising this dance for nearly a year. An international dance-off that was being done by some uplink video thing, Issy couldn't remember the technical stuff. If they won, it would mean that they could turn professional. *She* could turn professional. They wouldn't be able to send her back then. She was dancing in a British dance group, *British*. Issy would have preferred to do street dance, but someone had come up with the idea that the different countries should swap dances with each other. It was dumb. They'd been emailing each other to create a sense of cohesion. Whatever.

As she shimmied around the stage with the others, Issy thought about the story behind their dance. It was to do with poor villagers and no food or something like that. And how they'd sent their virgins out to plead with the gods. Like there'd be many of them hanging around waiting to do a dance. Issy's heart beat faster as she thought about the two solos she had to do. What if she messed up? What if the gods weren't pleased? She had to do it right. They all had to do it right, they had to win. Issy had to win.

Knowing it would come to this hadn't prepared her. It was like it was happening to someone else. She'd only been eight when they brought her to Manchester, travelling with someone who'd called herself aunty but disappeared as soon as they landed. Issy had looked for her, squeezing in between the stinking, sweating bodies that blocked her way, dodging the hands that would have slapped her, ignoring the shouts from scary old men. But the crowds thinned out and she still couldn't find aunty. She was on her own and she was scared.

Pushing out her arms, she flexed her body in time to the beat. The heat was rising now and she could feel the sweat trickling between her shoulder blades. Dipping low, she snaked her body upwards. It was a policewoman who'd come and taken her to a small grey room. She'd eaten doughnuts while she waited. They were covered in icing with pink and white flakes. That was the first time she'd ever tasted them. Back-to-back now, she sidestepped, bumping backsides and shoulder blades before taking one step forward.

Issy had lived here longer than she'd lived in Nigeria. This was her home. She didn't know her parents or her brothers and sisters. Her social worker had told her a few weeks ago that they'd managed to make contact. That she had a large family waiting for her back home. And how exciting was that? It was bullshit and they both knew it. Manchester was Issy's home. This was where she belonged.

Breathing deeply, she waited at the left-hand side of the stage for her first solo. They each took centre stage at different points throughout the dance. Issy was third. She kept her eyes fixed to the boards in front of her. It wasn't supposed to have been like that. Aunty should have passed her over to some guy waiting at the barrier when they came through. But something had gone wrong. The social worker said aunty had probably panicked. Maybe it was her first time, or maybe it had been the plan all along, they'd never know. But the fact was, Issy was abandoned at the airport with no passport.

The music altered as the soloist shimmied around the stage. She'd been taken to the emergency unit. Issy could still remember it. The low flat building had reminded her of the chief's house in her village. The thought startled her and she stumbled slightly. She didn't know she'd remembered that.

The second soloist took her place and a new rhythm vibrated around the theatre. There were too many corridors and glass doors and the boys had made fun of her. They spoke too fast and she couldn't understand them. Issy had cried for a long time. There was one lady, Jackie, who'd sat with her and held her hand. She was the nicest. And when she'd learnt enough England-English to understand what was going on, Jackie had warned her about the men that hung around outside. Had told her not to go out alone. That was a laugh. She could come all the way from Nigeria on her own but she couldn't go out the door of the place she was living. She'd been there for six months before they found her a family to live with. The tempo increased and Issy lunged across the stage throwing her arms forward and following with her body. Her feet moved, staccato, her hips twirled in frenzy as she took centre stage.

Her parents had sent her to work for some rich African family. She'd been bought, apparently. They'd received money for their eldest daughter. How could they do that? The lady who came from the refugee place had told her when she was about due to do her GCSEs. Her own parents had sold her. Pushing her chest out, Issy thumped out the beat, her breath becoming shallow. She'd tried to make it sound normal, the refugee woman, a thing that happened with poor families in her country, but Issy wouldn't listen. She hated them. They had no right to do that to her. She'd said that her parents wouldn't have known, perhaps they were paying a debt, perhaps they'd been promised a better life for Issy, with regular money being sent home. Perhaps it had been Issy's duty to do this for her family. Like fuck it was. Would she send her own daughter to another country if she needed some dosh? The music froze and Issy held her pose before the drum beat started again, softer this time, and she shimmied to the back of the stage while another dancer took her place.

Breathing heavily now, Issy waited for her body to calm down. The sweat was pouring into her eyes. They were stinging. She wiped around her mascara with the tips of her fingers. She could look out from where she was now, in the shadows. The audience was vague shapes rising like a tidal wave. To the left she could see her teacher moving in time to the beat. Two more solos to go.

The foster families were mostly ok. But luckily her first social worker had liked her and had worked really hard to find her somewhere she could stay long-term. It had taken five attempts before she'd been put with Molly, who cooked rice and peas and stew beans and mutton and oxtail. She'd stayed there until she was sixteen, had been part of the family. But then she'd had to move on. Those three years she'd spent with Molly and her family had been almost like belonging. But each time the family went on holiday she'd been placed somewhere else because Molly couldn't get her a passport so she could go with them.

Manchester Foyer had been the place to begin her independence. They'd meant it was the place for her to get used to being alone. The beat changed again as the solo dancers changed. It wouldn't be long now until Issy danced the finale. Her final plea to the faceless gods. It had been ok living there. She'd worked her way up to the top floor because she went to college every day, and didn't do drugs. She didn't even drink much. She couldn't if she wanted to take her dancing seriously. Her mate had introduced her to a guy who said he could help. Issy hadn't even known she needed help then. But it worked out she did. That she was being watched by the Home Office or something. She'd laughed when he said that. As if. As if anyone was interested in what she did. But he was serious. Said she was a foreigner. That she'd be sent home when she got to eighteen.

Her body was cooling down now. She stood in the shadows and waited for her final entrance. She'd chosen not to let the man help her. She didn't trust him, had heard the stories of girls ending up as prostitutes and shit, and there was no way that was gonna be her life. Her mates had turned against her a bit after that, said she was a snob, that she deserved to be sent back, that she'd change her mind. Issy had trusted her solicitor. She'd trusted the system. And it was like they'd both screwed her. The beat was picking up now, this was the part of the dance where the gods weren't happy and the drums were loud and the lights were flashing. The girls on stage were vibrating with the music, coming together and pushing apart. Issy had so looked forward to this bit. Hers was the main part.

As the music went lower, only for a few bars, Issy could feel the audience preparing to do something. She could feel the shift in their posture. Arms were unfolded and hands were freed from pockets, ready to applaud. This was the part she liked the best. This was when they were pushed back into their seats as the drumbeat became ferocious. The gods were displeased with the dances that had been offered. Now the group had to re-form, make an offering to appease them. Issy could feel the rhythm pulsing through her body, her heart beating longer and harder as the drum became part of her. Stomping in time, the girls came together in the middle of the stage. Pushing against each other they acted out the displeasure of the gods until the music felled them one by one and only Issy was left standing, head bowed, hands held out in supplication. If only, she thought as she raised her head and her arms, if only she could go in front of the judge herself and tell him.

Stepping away from the prostrate girls, Issy moved to the front of the stage. The drums were now a rumble in the background, the lights soft behind her. As the spotlight slowly brightened she began to appease the angry gods, to dance for their lives.

Standing at the front of the stage, she felt her foreignness pulling her down, the bureaucracy and policy wrapping itself around her like African cloth. As far back as she could remember, official people had decided where she should go, where she should live, which school she should go to. Issy had had enough. She twirled around the stage alternately bowing and preening, seducing the gods with a flick of her hips while looking demurely downwards, looking boldly forward while covering her body with her hands. Spreading her arms, she twirled and dipped, pulsing her thin body to the beat of the drums, oblivious to anything except the rhythm running through her.

The drumming slowed down and she reached centre stage, joining the other girls in a victory pose. Issy thought about her solicitor's last message. *Now we can appeal.*

The Curry Mile: Placing Taste, Tasting Place in Manchester

SARAH GIBSON

Zahid Hussain's novel, *The Curry Mile*, occupies a distinctive space within Britain's multicultural imaginary.[1] As a novel set in a number of restaurants along what is popularly known as the Curry Mile on Wilmslow Road in Manchester's Rusholme district, it tells the story of Sorayah Butt's return home from London, and explores her troubled relationship with her father, Ajmal, the 'Curry King' of Manchester. As the first published literary representation of the Curry Mile, the novel is a notable addition to the increasingly diverse articulations of black Britain. Indeed, the novel's very publication by Suitcase Books, the Manchester-based community press, disturbs the more familiar canon of black and diasporic writing that imagines Britain as 'a singularly undifferentiated setting'.[2] According to James Procter, this canon has predominantly focused on London and reflects what Corinne Fowler describes as 'the commercial and cultural logic by which novels are coded as worthy of national and international readerships by corporate publishers'.[3] This cultural logic racially remaps Britain's cultural landscape in such a way that London becomes the nucleus of multiracial Britain, while the North is nostalgically reimagined as the province of whiteness.[4] *The Curry Mile* thus articulates significant local and regional differences in the representation of black Britishness. Arguing that Hussain's depiction of the Curry Mile contributes to an understanding of the diversity of multicultural Britain, this article explores the way in which the novel's metaphorical use of food imagines Manchester as a 'glocal' city.[5] It argues that the novel's strategic use of gastronomic imagery allows it to be ambivalently positioned in relationship to the dominant discourse of culinary multiculturalism in Britain.

A Glocal Sense of Place

The passing of the nineteenth century has seen Manchester's transformation from a globalizing urban centre to the globalized city it is today.[6] Emerging during the industrial revolution, it can be described as

Britain's 'foremost *migrant* city'[7] because its ability to industrialize was dependent upon demographic flows from the English countryside as well as from Ireland, Eastern Europe and the former colonies. Given that its foundations rest upon immigration, Manchester is a prime example of what Corinne Fowler and Graham Mort describe as an 'imaginative domain … reflect[ing] a bewildering glocality of consciousness' as its meaning is constantly (re)inscribed by its architects, planners, builders, citizens, councillors and, of course, its creative writers.[8] One of the ways in which this glocal sense of place is constructed is through the hybridities of taste, cooking, and eating performed on this section of Wilmslow Road, a place famed for having the largest concentration of 'Indian'[9] restaurants in the country.

The transformation of Wilmslow Road into the Curry Mile began in the 1970s when South Asian-owned businesses catered to local BrAsians[10] who visited Rusholme for the cinemas that were screening Bollywood movies at the weekend. However it was only during the 1980s that the Curry Mile established itself as a place renowned for 'Indian' restaurants. This was owing to Manchester's increasing student population as well as to 'the growing popularity of BrAsian food among the white population'.[11]

Food has become pivotal to the glocal sense of Manchester today.[12] Not only do specific dishes originate from specific places but they also symbolically reconstruct those locations.[13] The Curry Mile is a distinctive place that both reflects and performs the complex 'food mobilities' associated with colonialism, migration, and tourism.[14] As Sorayah comments in the novel, 'look how much Manchester has changed just because of apna food' (p. 102) and the Curry Mile is described as being '*only in Manchester*' (p. 47). It is through the use of food metaphors that the novel draws attention to the specific '*local migrations*' in Manchester.[15] While 'Indian' restaurants in Britain are commonly associated with Sylheti migrants from Bangladesh, restaurants on the Curry Mile are instead associated with BrAsians from Pakistan, a fact that reflects Manchester's distinctive histories of migration.[16] The restaurants along the Curry Mile are an illustration of the local articulation of what Ian Cook and Phil Crang describe as the 'globally extensive networks and flows of foods, people and culinary knowledge'.[17]

Hussain's novel is set within an identifiably Mancunian landscape with archetypal landmarks, such as the Siemens Building, Southern Cemetery, Hulme Arch, and the Mancunian Way. Crucially, though, the Curry Mile is integral to this landscape. On her return home to Manchester from

London, Sorayah views the restaurants and takeaways as familiar sights/ sites, which are used to communicate the Curry Mile's glocal sense of place:

> Even before they hit Wilmslow Road, she spied her first Abdul's Takeaway of the day. … Then out of the traffic at Oxford Road, neon crowns dimmed by daylight. Sorayah knew them all. They chanted their names to her: Sanam, Sangam, Shere Khan, Tabbak, Hanaant, Royal Naz, Tandoori Kitchen, Shezan, Lal Haweli, Lal Qila, Dildar, Darbar, Kashmir, Maharajaah, Curry Wala and the Spice Hut. (pp. 46-47)

For Hussain, the Curry Mile both 'defines Manchester' and 'the reality of modern day Britain' and, he goes on to argue, the Curry Mile is 'an incredible location for a novel' that is 'definitely equal if not better than Brick Lane'.[18] It is a unique place for articulating what Hussain terms 'modern multicultural Bombay-mix Britain' (p. 13) with its heterogeneous population of 'university students, college students, restaurant and takeaway workers, newsagents, Pakistanis, Arabs, Kurds, Indians, Jamaicans [and] Somalis'.[19] In writing *The Curry Mile*, Hussain constructs Manchester as the multicultural metropolis, displacing both London's status as the 'cultural capital of black Britain'[20] and Brick Lane's position as the nation's 'curry capital'.[21] The preoccupation of much mainstream twenty-first-century fiction with multiracial London has been at the expense of 'a more complex, regionally focused, understanding of the diasporic experience in Britain today'.[22] *The Curry Mile* is an important contribution to the 'increasingly regional, locally accented black British literature'[23] located outside of London in its representation of 'modern-day Britain through the eyes of Mancunian Pakistanis'.[24] As a review in the *Guardian* noted, the novel is 'an enjoyable slice of Desi life, Manchester style'.[25]

Culinary Multiculturalism

Before focusing on the use of gastronomic imagery in *The Curry Mile*, however, it is necessary to provide a brief background to the study of food, identity, and community. As Terry Eagleton writes, 'if there is one sure thing about food, it is never just food.'[26] Roland Barthes argues that food is 'a system of communication' and that 'an entire "world" (social environment) is present in and signified by food', and Arjun Appadurai concurs that food is a 'marvellously plastic kind of collective representation'.[27] Food is central to communicating identities, whether national, regional, gendered, religious, ethnic or classed identities. Cultures of food and eating are an important way of defining identity and difference between us and them, self and other, and in definitions of the edible and inedible, taste and disgust.[28] As Lynette Hunter argues, 'food has a way of bringing people together and also of keeping them apart'.[29] Food, and what counts as food, is thus both a 'way of placing oneself in relation to others' and a way of imagining a shared cultural community.[30]

Above all, food has become central to the discourse of British multiculturalism.[31] A notable realization of this phenomenon was Robin Cook's (in)famous naming of Chicken Tikka Masala as Britain's national dish in 2001.[32] In rhetoric such as this, culinary diversity becomes a 'distinguishing characteristic of contemporary Britishness'.[33] Most notably, it is 'Indian' food that is described as an integral part of Britain's culinary culture.[34] 'Indian' food, or 'curry', has a long and complex history in the construction of British identity from colonial times to the present day. In the discourse of culinary multiculturalism, food becomes appropriated as a symbol of Britain's diversity but only in so far as it is positioned as different, spicy, and exotic. As a typical exponent of this stance, Christina Hardyment regards the presence of 'Indian' restaurants on the British High Street as a positive symbol of British multiculturalism, as a 'celebration of difference rather than obsessive integration'.[35]

One of the most regular criticisms of the construction of multiculturalism through culinary culture and food is that it maintains the boundaries between different social groups. Criticized as a way of what bell hooks terms 'eating the other', ethnicity is constructed as exotic by means of a food analogy where it is the white Western consumer who is 'invited to "go ethnic" through what she or he might eat'.[36] The taste for ethnic food is read as 'cultural food colonialism', where the taste for ethnic food is motivated by and perpetuates the power relations of colonialism.[37] As Anne-Marie Fortier argues, culinary multiculturalism is a 'fantasy of multicultural intimacy', where 'the circulation of "ethnicity" as a "taste" … celebrates and consumes diversity alongside the devaluation of the physical and political presence of migrants. … The migrant-as-ethnic is invited *on*, not *at*, the kitchen table'.[38] In Ghassan Hage's words, this is consumer orientated multiculturalism 'without the migrants'.[39]

The Curry Mile has a complex and contradictory relationship to this dominant discourse of culinary multiculturalism in Britain as it participates in 'the general cultural currency of the "curry" in Britain'.[40] The title places the novel within familiar culinary imagery associated with multiculturalism in its evocation of both the taste of place (curry) and the place of taste (the Curry Mile). Since food is apparently situated here as both 'exotic' and 'ethnic', this could of course be read as a sign of a 'staged marginality', whereby 'marginalised individuals or social groups are moved to dramatise their "subordinate" status for the benefit of a majority or mainstream audience'.[41] In such a reading, the novel would be considered as complicit in the discourse of culinary multiculturalism and postcolonial exoticism, making them palatable to a wide readership.[42] However, although *The Curry Mile* arguably exoticizes itself for a mainstream audience by strategically playing with gastronomic imagery, the use of food metaphors throughout the novel suggests a more critical stance towards the commodification of difference. Food in the novel is not straightforwardly equated to exoticism since it also draws attention to the banal acts of eating and cooking 'Indian' food in the performance of BrAsian identity. Similarly, by representing 'Indian' food from the perspective of those working in the restaurant, the invisible 'back-stage' world of the 'Indian' restaurant is foregrounded, in clear contrast to its frequent erasure in consumer orientated models of multiculturalism.[43]

Food becomes both exotic *and* mundane in the novel, and it is this tension circulating between what Huggan terms the 'postcolonial exotic' and Procter identifies as the 'postcolonial everyday' that confounds any straightforward equation between food, ethnicity, and authenticity. As Procter notes, 'one audience's exotic is another's everyday'.[44] What is exotic about 'Indian' food for a white British audience is familiar, homely, and mundane for diasporic migrant communities and delighted in for these reasons. As such, while the novel self-consciously constructs multicultural Britain in culinary terms, this is not the same as simply reproducing colonialist stereotypes: it is instead, I wish to argue, 'a skilled manipulation' of the 'postcolonial exotic'.[45] Indeed, *The Curry Mile* critiques the discourse of culinary multiculturalism through its setting in both the domestic family kitchen as well as the 'Indian' restaurant.

The 'Postcolonial Everyday': Home Cooking

The home, or 'dwelling place', is an important location for the representation of black Britishness.[46] In *The Curry Mile*, food metaphors are central to the construction of both the family home and the diasporic homeland. '*Home*', Sorayah comments upon her return to Rusholme, '*is where the dil is*' (p. 49). In contrast to the cooking of food within the restaurant, the family and the homeland are produced through the gendered divisions of labour within the home, particularly in relation to cooking. It is the cooking and eating of homemade food within the domestic household that problematizes the dominant myth of 'Indian' food in Britain. The Butts' home is to begin with presented as reflecting gendered stereotypes, where the housewife's cooking reproduces the 'home and family'[47] as well as the diasporic homeland. Mumtaz is initially positioned within the home as a nostalgic 'cooking woman'[48] who serves her husband, Ajmal:

> His restaurants were renowned for the exquisite sensations they aroused, but nothing matched his wife's cooking. Mumtaz was making parata and his favourite morning snack, fried andey with onions, chillies and of course, garam masala. (p. 29)

Mumtaz's home-made food is invested with love and care, and is opposed to the mass produced food of the restaurant: her food is 'fresh as a newborn baby' (p. 29).

The cooking of food from the homeland is thus associated with the domestic kitchen, where cooking is central to 'migrant home-building practices'.[49] Having arrived in Britain during the 1960s, Ajmal, for example, is discerning about his cup of tea. While the English cup of tea is described as 'filthy watery English chaa', by contrast the Pakistani tea he drinks is the 'soothing nectar that refreshed his immigrant lips' (p. 53). While Mumtaz is associated with cooking food, Ajmal is associated with eating it: 'his mouth enjoy[ing] the layered textures and tastes' (p. 29).

When Sorayah returns home to Manchester, her mother cooks her favourite meal of 'lamb curry and carrot halwa' (p. 51) by way of a greeting. Initially, Sorayah is presented as being welcomed by the memories that such food provokes: '[as she] smelt the rich aroma of the lamb curry … a flood of smells washed over her: sweet, aromatic, fiery, bitter-sweet, earthy, hot and intoxicating' (p. 72). However, this equation of home with food and nostalgia for her mother's cooking is quickly disrupted by another memory: 'it felt odd. Her mother had never cooked for her. Her ammi used to rise early to cook breakfast for Shokat and Imran, but never for her' (p. 72). Clearly it is again the males who are cooked for; but crucially, I want to argue, the novel here challenges the equation of gender with cooking in the home. In *The Curry Mile*, cooking is not a skill passed down from mother to daughter.[50] Sorayah learns to cook not in the maternal space of the mother's kitchen but in 'her father's restaurants' (p. 48). 'More at home in a restaurant than anywhere else' (p. 36), she is only ever depicted as cooking in the restaurant kitchen. Rather than Sorayah's 'feeding work' producing the home and family,[51] her cooking is entrepreneurial, as she 'absorb[s] how to balance a ledger, order meat, hire workers' (p. 48).

Sorayah's hybridized identity is represented through her taste in food. In contrast to her father's migrant tastes, Sorayah relishes eating 'tandoori chicken and lamb kebabs smothered in ketchup', 'mint tea, baklava, and shisha' and 'tasteless supermarket branded cornflakes' (pp. 117, 178, 120). Likewise the egg dish she cooks fuses the traditional British 'omelette' with the 'pizzazz' of spices.

> She took her time, fried the onions until they were brown and tender. […] She nicked the eggs expertly on the edge of the frying pan. They cracked, spilling their contents into the pan, and she threw the shells into the large bin without looking. Salt and garam masala followed, then chillies to give it pizzazz. (p. 242)

Finally, this representation of Sorayah cooking for her friend, Shabnam, produces a space of female friendship rather than that of the patriarchal home and family. As the cooking of BrAsian food by Sorayah in the novel mirrors the performance of her own hybridized identity as a BrAsian, so a questions she asks is: '*Am I still the same British-born confused Desi?*' (p. 35).

The 'Postcolonial Exotic': The 'Indian' Restaurant

Hussain's novel offers a critique of celebratory culinary multiculturalism by representing 'the restaurant trade' as a competitive 'cut-throat world' (p. 26). By drawing attention to the labour involved in creating, marketing, and sustaining a desire to eat ethnic food by a wide range of consumers, the restaurant setting challenges the 'eater-centred' discourse of culinary multiculturalism that frequently erases 'ethnic feeders' from view.[52] As Uma Narayan argues, it is important to think about 'ethnic foods from the point of view of immigrants to western contexts, rather than that of mainstream western citizens … [since] the desire for culinary novelty mak[es] a positive difference to profit margins'.[53] It is not simply a question of 'eating the other', but also of who is feeding the consumers.

The 'feeding work' that Marjorie DeVault identifies in terms of gendered identities is constructed here along ethnic lines. Ajmal Butt is presented as profiting from the taste for ethnic food by white consumers: his restaurants 'were sprouting up everywhere to feed the insatiable indigenous goray's appetite for ex-colonial cuisine' (p. 85). Sorayah's brother, Shokat Butt, who is described in the novel as 'the behind the scenes guy', for example, 'instinctively knew how much a prawn karahi should cost, if chicken dopiaza should be on offer or if the popadoms should be free' (p. 44) in order to attract custom. Indeed, culinary multiculturalism is strategically articulated by staff as a promotional tool. Ajmal, for example, had 'appeared on countless documentaries and loved to talk about how curry was "allowing everyone to come closer." *That's total bakwaas, but the goray love to hear it.* His apna food fed the masses and cost mere pennies to make' (p. 55).

The Curry Mile draws a clear distinction between the food cooked at home and the food cooked inside the restaurant. As represented in the novel, the food served in the restaurant is important for its critique of the postcolonial exotic and culinary multiculturalism. As well as underlining the profit-making concerns of the restaurant, the novel challenges the ignorance of those 'food adventurers'[54] associated with eating ethnic food: 'the idiots burn half of it and those goray eat it any way thinking that's how it's meant to be. Charcoal. Silly people' (p. 175). It also foregrounds the inauthenticity of the food cooked and eaten within such 'Indian' restaurants. Being far outside the everyday, the food is as 'exotic' to Sorayah and her friends as it is to the local 'white' community:

> 'What's the difference between a jalfrezi and a dopsanda again?' Shabnam asked. … She found herself explaining how curries were made. She explained why curries 'don't taste like ammi's cooking,' and why 'the gorays love it so much.' (p. 102)

Culinary multiculturalism is also parodied in the novel from the perspective of those working in the restaurant:

> The good food here is about bringing the world together. … This is where we see fruits of Asian culture mixing with the local white people. … You know, my children they eat fish'n'chips just like their white friends, but they also love to eat curry, just like their white friends, so tell me are we any different from each other? How can we be different if we have the same taste in the wonderful food? (p. 236)

The novel identifies binary oppositions between local white and Asian, fish and chips and curry, but the narrative disrupts these dichotomies by suggesting that Britishness, and the British diet, is constructed through a taste for both fish and chips and curry.

Reading *The Curry Mile*

Hussain's novel uses food as a way of exploring the tension between Huggan's 'postcolonial exotic' and Procter's 'postcolonial everyday'. Food's 'polysemia'[55] is used strategically in order to refuse any simplistic reading of food's meaning and role in imagining identity, culture, and community in Britain today. Lisa Heldke argues that 'the challenge of food anticolonialism is to develop ways of approaching food that … cultivate an openness to otherness without objectifying them or treating them as resources from which to support one's own lifestyle'.[56] The use of food metaphors in *The Curry Mile* similarly encourages a more complex and historically contextualized reading of food in a multicultural society, denying the reader any stable point of identification, and defamiliarizing the depiction of food and the space of consumption (the restaurant) in the discourse of culinary multiculturalism.

In its articulation of both a Mancunian and a British glocal sense of place, *The Curry Mile* draws attention to both the regional and national multicultural imaginary. While at the start of the novel London is positioned as Manchester's exotic other as it 'pulsated to a different Asian rhythm' (p. 49), the novel also celebrates the glocality of Manchester as it becomes '*more like London*' (p. 47). This 'dynamic space'[57] of the Curry Mile is epitomized when, instead of nostalgically looking back to 'the heyday of the curry trade' (p. 85), Sorayah positively embraces the fact that there were now 'Iranian, Arab, Jamaican restaurants fused into the predominantly Pakistani-owned businesses' (p. 192). The Curry Mile is thus a 'progressive sense of place',[58] whose meaning is constructed through the constantly changing hybridities of taste, cooking, and eating performed on Wilmslow Road.

NOTES

Thanks to Dawn Llewellyn and Fiona Doloughan for reading drafts of this article. My thanks also go to Corinne Fowler for her helpful suggestions and for sharing her research with me.

1. Zahid Hussain, *The Curry Mile* (London: Suitcase Books, 2006). All further references are to this edition and are included in the text.
2. James Procter, *Dwelling Places: Postwar Black British Writing* (Manchester: Manchester UP, 2003), p. 1.
3. Corinne Fowler, 'A Tale of Two Novels: Developing a Devolved Approach to Black British Writing', *Journal of Commonwealth Writing*, 43:3 (2008) 75-94, p. 76.
4. James Procter, 'The Postcolonial Everyday', *New Formations*, 58 (2006) 62-80, p. 73.
5. Doreen Massey argues that 'a global sense of place' is one that positively integrates the global and the local *Space, Place, and Gender* (Cambridge: Polity, 1994), pp. 146-56. Roland Robertson uses the term 'glocalization' in order to draw attention to the interconnections of the global and the local, 'Glocalization: Time-Space and Homogeneity–Heterogeneity', in *Global Modernities*, eds, Mike Featherstone, Scott Lash and Roland Robertson (London: Sage, 1995), pp. 25-44.
6. Peter Dicken, 'Global Manchester', in *City of Revolution: Restructuring Manchester*, eds, Jamie Peck and Kevin Ward (Manchester: Manchester UP, 2002), pp. 18-33.
7. Corinne Fowler and Lynne Pearce, 'Moving Manchester: Relocating Diaspora Research', *International Journal of the Humanities*, 4:6 (2006) 93-100, p. 93.
8. Corinne Fowler and Graham Mort, 'The Politics of Method', *International Journal of the Arts in Society*, 1:7 (2007) 1-8, p. 2.
9. The food that is popularly known as 'Indian' is a fabrication which erases regional histories of cooking. The word 'curry' is thought to derive from the Tamil word *kari*. Even though the word originates from India, 'curry' itself is a British invention. See Lisa Heldke, *Exotic Appetites* (London: Routledge, 2003), pp. 34-49. Uma Narayan equates the invention of 'curry' with the invention of 'India' as a unitary signifier and

political entity. See 'Eating Cultures: Incorporation, Identity and Indian Food', *Social Identities*, 1:1 (1995) 63-86, p. 65. Also see Nurpur Chaudhuri, 'Shawls, Jewelry, Curry and Rice in Victorian Britain', in *Western Women and Imperialism: Complicity and Resistance*, eds, Nurpur Chaudhuri and M. Strobel (Bloomington: Indiana UP, 1992), pp. 231-46 and Susan Zlotnick, 'Domesticating Imperialism: Curry and Cookbooks in Victorian England', *Frontiers*, 16:2/3 (1996) 51-68.

10. The term 'BrAsian' refers to 'members of settler communities which articulate a significant part of their identity in terms of South Asian heritage', Salman Sayyid, 'Introduction: BrAsians: Postcolonial People, Ironic Citizens', in *A Postcolonial People: South Asians in Britain*, eds, Nasreen Ali, Virinder S. Kalra, and Salman Sayyid (London: Hurst, 2006), pp. 1-10 (p. 5).

11. Nida Kirmani, 'Rusholme', in *A Postcolonial People: South Asians in Britain*, pp. 327-28.

12. David Bell, 'What's Eating Manchester? Gastro-Culture and Urban Regeneration', *Architectural Design*, 75:3 (2005) 78-85.

13. Ian Cook and Phil Crang, 'The World on a Plate: Culinary Culture, Displacement and Geographical Knowledges', *Journal of Material Culture*, 1:2 (1996) 131-153, p. 140.

14. Sarah Gibson, 'Food Mobilities: Traveling, Dwelling, and Eating Cultures', *Space and Culture*, 10:1 (2007) 4-21, p. 16.

15. Susheila Nasta, *Home Truths: Fictions of the South Asian Diaspora in Britain* (Basingstoke: Palgrave, 2001), p. 181.

16. Giles A. Barrett and David McEvoy, 'The Evolution of Manchester's Curry Mile', *Landscapes of the Ethnic Economy*, eds, David H. Kaplan and Wei Li (Plymouth: Rowman and Littlefield, 2006), pp. 193-207 (p. 195). On Manchester's distinct migration history, see Pnina Werbner, *Imagined Diasporas among Manchester Muslims* (Oxford: James Currey, 2002); and *The Migration Process* (London: Berg, 2002); and *Pilgrims of Love* (Indiana: Indiana UP, 2004).

17. Cook and Crang, 'The World on a Plate', p. 132.

18. Zahid Hussain, 'Writing the Curry Mile', <http://www.bbc.co.uk/manchester/content/articles/2006/10/16/161006_curry_mile_feature.shtml> accessed 11 July 2008.

19. Hussain, 'Writing the Curry Mile.'

20. Procter, *Dwelling Places*, p. 164.

21. Sean Carey, *Curry Capital: The Restaurant Sector in London's Brick Lane* (London: Institute of Community Studies, 2004).

22. Fowler and Pearce, 'Moving Manchester: Relocating Diaspora Research', p. 97.

23. Procter, *Dwelling Places*, p. 164.

24. Sarah Athey and Zahid Hussain, 'Zahid's love for literature', <http://www.bbc.co.uk/manchester/content/articles/2006/10/16/161006_curry_mile_feature.shtml> accessed 11 July 2008.

25. Rachel Hore, 'Glorious Debuts', *Guardian*, 2 December 2006, Guardian Review Pages, p. 17.

26. Terry Eagleton, 'Edible Écriture', in *Consuming Passions: Food in the Age of Anxiety*, eds, Sian Griffiths and Jennifer Wallace (Manchester: Manchester UP, 1998), pp. 203-08 (p. 204).

27. Roland Barthes, 'Towards a Psychosociology of Contemporary Food Consumption', in *Food and Culture: A Reader*, eds, Carole Counihan and Penny Van Esterik (London: Routledge, 1997), pp. 20-27 (p. 23). Arjun Appadurai, 'Gastro-Politics in Hindu South Asian', *American Ethnologist*, 8:3 (1981) 494-511, p. 494.

28. Pasi Falk, *The Consuming Body* (London: Sage, 1994), p. 69.

29. Lynette Hunter, 'Editorial', *Moving Worlds*, 6:2 (2006).

30. Jack Goody, *Cooking, Cuisine and Class* (Cambridge: Cambridge UP, 1982), p. 37.
31. Ian Cook, Phil Crang, and Mark Thorpe, 'Eating into Britishness: Multicultural Imaginaries and the Identity Politics of Food', in *Practising Identities: Power and Resistance*, eds, Sasha Roseneil and Julie Seymour (London: Macmillan, 1999), pp. 223-48 (p. 246).
32. Robin Cook, 'Robin Cook's Chicken Tikka Masala Speech', 19 April 2001 <http://www.guardian.co.uk/world/2001/apr/19/race.britishidentity> accessed 11 March 2009. The myth of what I term the 'Masala of Britishness' is implicitly critiqued in *The Curry Mile* when chicken tikka masala is described as 'tasteless' (p. 211). The dish that is heralded as 'a celebration of Britain's multiculturalism', Jo Monroe, *Star of India: The Spicy Adventures of Curry* (Chichester: Wiley, 2005), p. 3, is considered as insipid within Manchester.
33. Cook, Crang and Thorpe, 'Eating into Britishness', p. 225.
34. Mark Leonard, *BritainTM: Renewing Our Identity* (London: Demos, 1997), p. 57.
35. Christina Hardyment, *Slice of Life: The British Way of Eating since 1945* (London: BBC Books, 1995), p. 122.
36. bell hooks, *Black Looks: Race and Representation* (London: South End Press, 1992), pp. 21-39. Sara Ahmed, *Strange Encounters* (London: Routledge, 2000), pp. 116-17. hooks argues that with the commodification of otherness, 'ethnicity becomes spice, seasoning that can liven up the dull dish that is mainstream white culture' (p. 21). It is through 'eating the other' that the consumer 'asserts power and privilege' (p. 36).
37. Heldke, *Exotic Appetites*, p. xv.
38. Anne-Marie Fortier, *Multicultural Horizons* (London: Routledge, 2007), pp. 91-93. This circulation of ethnicity as a taste has been noted by Graham Huggan who argues that India 'is more available than ever for consumption, and more prevalent than ever are the gastronomic images through which the nation is to be consumed', *The Postcolonial Exotic* (London: Routledge, 2001), p. 82.
39. Ghassan Hage, 'At Home in the Entrails of the West', in *Home/World: Space, Community and Marginality in Sydney's West*, eds, Helen Grace, Ghassan Hage, Lesley Johnson, Julie Langsworth, and Michael Symonds (Annandale, New South Wales: Pluto, 1997), pp. 99-153 (p. 100).
40. Ben Highmore, 'Alimentary Agents: Food, Cultural Theory and Multiculturalism', *Journal of Intercultural Studies*, 29:4 (2008) 381-98, p. 382.
41. Huggan, *The Postcolonial Exotic*, p. 87.
42. Hussain reflects that the novel went through several titles as it was being redrafted: *Abrasion*, *The Curry King*, *Sorayah's Song*, and finally *The Curry Mile*, commenting that through this redrafting 'the writing has been homogenised into a more commercial and palatable whole', Zahid Hussain, private email to Corinne Fowler, 21 August 2008.
43. The concept of 'back stage' and 'front stage' regions emerges from the work of Erving Goffman, where he uses the example of the kitchen and the dining room in a restaurant, *The Presentation of Self in Everyday Life* (Harmondsworth: Penguin, 1990), pp. 123-24.
44. Procter, 'The Postcolonial Everyday', p. 65.
45. Mark Stein, 'Curry at Work: Nibbling at the Jewel in the Crown', in *Eating Culture: The Poetics and Politics of Food*, eds, Tobias Döring, Markus Heide and Susanne Mühleisen (Heidelberg: Universitatsverlag, 2003), pp. 133-49 (p. 147).
46. Procter, *Dwelling Places*, p. 4.
47. Marjorie DeVault, *Feeding the Family* (London: U of Chicago P, 1991), p. 79.
48. Jean Duruz, 'Haunted Kitchens: Cooking and Remembering', *Gastronomica*, 4:1 (2004)

57-68, p. 61.

49. Hage, 'At Home in the Entrails of the West', p. 100.
50. Luce Giard, 'Doing Cooking', in *The Practice of Everyday Life Volume 2: Living and Cooking*, eds, Michel de Certeau, Luce Giard, and Pierre Mayol (London: U of Minnesota P, 1998), pp. 149-249.
51. DeVault, *Feeding the Family*, pp. 90-91.
52. Hage, 'At Home in the Entrails of the West', p. 118.
53. Narayan, 'Eating Cultures: Incorporation, Identity and Indian Food', p. 76.
54. Heldke, *Exotic Appetites*, p. xxi.
55. Barthes, 'Towards a Psychosociology of Contemporary Food Consumption', p. 25.
56. Heldke, *Exotic Appetites*, p. 168.
57. Kirmani, 'Rusholme', p. 328.
58. Massey, *Space, Place, and Gender*, p. 151.

MONIZA ALVI

Elsewhere

The flies row out in tiny boats.
Save digression, save the goats.
The King of Elsewhere on his knees.
Seven storms and seven seas.

Elsewhere with its awkward star,
far and near, near and far.

The lines of latitude are flowing,
white-haired winds are blowing, blowing.
Decisions made – the shock reverse.
Nothing wants, but dies of thirst.

All the elsewheres that we are.
The spider weaving at the bar.

Arms hook round a troubled name.
Through the woods the wisemen came.
Tend it well, or stop the gap,
a country on and off the map.

Elsewhere with its awkward star,
far and near, near and far.

Elsewhere crawling into view.
Mirror-shades are what we do.
A cherry-bite, a dispensation.
The dizziness. A dwindling nation.

All the elsewheres that we are.
The spider weaving at the bar.

The grey clouds of a waterfall
in front, behind us, not at all.
The crashing of the youngest son.
An heirloom necklace weighs a ton.

Elsewhere with its awkward star,
far and near, near and far.

The King of Elsewhere knows you not,
remembered once, and twice forgot.
Elsewhere, close to where you are.
Elsewhere with its door ajar.

All the elsewheres that we are.
The spider weaving at the bar.

Somewhere claims to be a place.
A second cousin in disgrace.
The trees are looping out of view.
Best check every part of you.

Elsewhere, with its awkward star,
far and near and near and far.
All the elsewheres that we are.
The spider weaving at the bar.

In Space

AFTER JULES SUPERVIELLE'S '47 BOULEVARD LANNES'

Wimbledon Park, what are you doing up there in space
with your milk vans and your four-by-fours,
dogs in the rec., noses pointing to the ground,
your hairdressers, your Chinese-style Indian restaurant –
everything so earthly?

Wimbledon Park, what are you doing in the middle of the sky,
the years sniffing at your terraced houses?
You're so remote from the London cloud and sun,
the streetlights don't know what to do.
And the milkman asks himself
if they really are houses
moving towards him,
with real gardens,
and if these are milk bottles or worlds
clinking in his fingers?
The sweeper of dead leaves
makes a pile for the common grave
of all the suburban trees spaced out in the sky.
The sweeping sounds huge –
a noise souls would love to imitate.
And the infants in class
comparing the colours of each other's hands,
are they still living, breathing children?

I doubt if Wolseley Avenue is any wider
than the distance between two stars.
If I place my ear
to a residential road
I hear the clashing of worlds,
the dizzying battles.
Through a crack in the pavement
I see a star trapped
by its own violence,
the elusive air
escaping on all sides.

I'm hidden behind a piece of night
as if it were a wall,
hushing my loud memory,
looking out with my human eyes
that have come all this way
in my masked face.

I can see clearly that it's this year,
but it could be the first day of the world,
so many things stare, shocked, at themselves.
I recognize my footsteps going off into the distance,
losing themselves by the lake in the park.
If I cry out, nobody hears anything –
just the groaning of the Earth
fingering her sphere, reminding herself
she still has mountains, rivers, forests,
She tends a bonfire
where the future warms itself, awaiting its turn.

I am alone with my confusion.
Where is she going between two skies
so far from solid Earth,
her thoughts crumpled?

Since I recognize the front of our house
I'll place a black and white photograph
of my mother and father, their two nations,
on a mantelpiece carved from this hard night.
Some researcher, discovering them up here,
will ponder over them forever.

But it'll be a long time
before my hand can come and go,
lacking of air, light and friends
in this aching sky
weakly moaning to itself
beneath the burden of all things
which have climbed up from the Earth.

Changing Identities, Changing Spaces: The Ferham Families Exhibition in Rotherham

KATE PAHL with ANDY POLLARD and ZAHIR RAFIQ

The Ferham Families project was an exhibition of narratives and objects from the homes of a group of five families who all lived in the Ferham area of Rotherham, South Yorkshire. The project was part of the Diasporas, Migration, Identities research programme, funded by the Arts and Humanities Research Council with additional funding from Creative Partnerships.[1] The project ran from January 2006 to March 2007. The research team included Kate Pahl, University of Sheffield (principal investigator), Andy Pollard, Sheffield Hallam University (curator and researcher), and Zahir Rafiq (artist and advisor to the project). The project team worked in partnership with Ferham School and Rotherham Central Sure Start to create an exhibition with Clifton Park Museum, the local museum in Rotherham. These partnerships enabled us to ensure that the project included parents and children from the local community.

The project aimed to explore which objects were special to families of Pakistani origin who lived in the Ferham area, and to investigate the stories that they could tell about their family history. A series of interviews with four members of one family and their children and one other family produced a wealth of historical and cultural material, which was then turned into an exhibition in Rotherham Art Gallery during April 2007. Zahir Rafiq also held a series of workshops with the children to create a digital presentation, which was then uploaded on to a website, that also includes family stories and objects. This website is now called Every Object Tells a Story (www.everyobjecttellsastory.org.uk). In addition, a Women's Art project, held at Rotherham Central Sure Start, provided artistic images for the exhibition, and Zahir Rafiq's contemporary Islamic art was also exhibited. This article partly takes the form of an interview which Kate Pahl conducted with Zahir Rafiq and Andy Pollard to explore, firstly, the nature of the project with a particular focus on changing British Asian identities within Rotherham; and secondly, the way in which Zahir Rafiq responded to these changes as an artist and specifically in his work for the Ferham Families project. It also draws on

Ferham Families exhibition. © Steve Wright

interviews with the families about the area they grew up in, and about objects and stories that were important to them.

Zahir was initially asked to do a website and to design a visual presentation to be incorporated into the final exhibition. He also worked with Andy Pollard to design the display boards for the final exhibition. He was in an advisory role on the project and was the link for the project with the families. Andy interviewed the families with Kate Pahl and analysed the data. He worked with family members to coordinate the identification and collection of objects, and to discover from interview scripts such themes as could be used to make sense of the diverse range of artefacts collected. He planned the space and curated the exhibition. Kate's role was to coordinate the project with the school and the family learning officer, Wendy Leak, at Sure Start, and to develop the educational and academic outcomes of the project. Kate and Wendy developed a Women's Art Project which involved working with a group of women of Pakistani heritage who provided art materials for the exhibition. She also conducted the interviews, and analysed the data with Andy. Andy and Kate have written an article about the project (Pahl and Pollard 2008) and, funded by the University of Sheffield, Kate put together from the stories and images a learning resources pack called 'Every Object Tells a Story'.

Children's toys. © Steve Wright

Intergenerational meanings

A key part of the project was that it involved three generations of one extended family. Its members consisted of two parents, who had migrated from the Pashtun regions of Pakistan in the 1960s to settle in Rotherham, their grown-up children, now settled in the Ferham area, and their grandchildren, who are in their early teens. The transitions and transformations of these different individuals across the generations and across two countries was central to the exhibition. All the families were involved in the design of the website, and the children donated their toys to the exhibition. Enduring artefacts, practices, and values handed down over time, such as gold, weddings, and family heritage were explored in the project and displayed in the exhibition together with contemporary objects. The exhibition also focused on current identities and practices that the children engaged with, such as football, toys, wrestling and computer games. The resulting exhibition was a mix of old and new. For example, the toys the children brought in were displayed alongside the Family Koran.

The Ferham area in Rotherham

When they were growing up, all the families interviewed for the project lived in the Ferham area of Rotherham, an area that is now bisected by a large motorway but remains a relatively tranquil area of Victorian-style

terraced housing, with a large school, Ferham Primary School, a Sure
Start, and a local park further up the road. It is an area that in the 1960s
was attractive to live in although the family was in a minority as being
from Pakistan,

> Oh, when we first came there weren't that many people on Ferham Road ... And
> now I think if you check Ferham it's predominantly Pakistanis and fewer English
> families, do you know what I mean? At that time we were the only two or three
> families here.[2]

The area had an old-fashioned feel, with small shops and an elderly
population,

> It was OK, there wasn't any problems ...There were a lot of old folks and like sort of
> grandmothers and older parents who are still alive and they have a different view
> about life in general[3]

However, at the point of doing the Ferham Families project, the family
had elected to sell up, as they felt that the area was changing,

> There were still a lot of people here that we knew, there were quite a lot of Asian
> families settled here by then of course and we knew a lot of people here, gradually
> for the next 10 years, I think it's just gradually changed, people begin to rent properties
> out, came in, the whole atmosphere. And I think also because a lot of people moved
> away so different people moved in which wasn't the same people, same calibre of
> people, it changed. And this area particularly became derelict, you know, went
> downhill.[4]

One key characteristic of the area was that when the families moved in,
many of them knocked two houses into one, to make the small, Victorian
terraced houses more capacious for big families,

> We bought this house, this one next door to us, at that time – it was about 20 years
> ago literally, we bought it. And I remember, because I used to be into DIY, I love
> doing things and my father used to, I would help him when I was very young and I
> used to do it myself and we knocked it through … the house.[5]

One informant, from a different family, said that the settled nature of
Ferham had kept her grandmother from moving back to Pakistan in her
old age,

> she gets on with everyone around here she talked about moving but she would never
> do that now, you would think she would want to move back to Pakistan where she
> was born, they have got houses there, you know everyone wants to make a fresh start
> but she doesn't like the idea now, although she was born there, I think the area, Ferham
> in itself, she wouldn't like to move out of there now, I feel I am part of this area now.[6]

The area and its feel was reflected in the publicity that Zahir produced for the project in which a street of houses, Victorian in style, is depicted. This community was quiet, settled, and, as Zahir remarked, 'Coronation Street' like. The families in the project had a great affection for the area. One family member had even designed some of the local traffic systems in his role as town-planner for Rotherham, and would show them off to his relatives.

> I used to drive them round and they know the area I used to drive through 'uncle designed that' and of course those signals, those traffic lights, they used to say to me as a bit of a laugh.[7]

The families in the exhibition saw themselves as part of the history of Ferham, and the exhibition reflected their profound affection for the area.

> I mean there are people like us who have been here historically as well there, so they have quite a stable place, a stable life, so it helps.[8]

Ferham Families as an exploration of contemporary British Asian identities

Central to the project's appeal was its focus on contemporary Islamic identities across generations, but also the commonalities between the communities in Rotherham. A series of long, extended interviews with the families then created key themes. These were discussed with the families. As a result of the interviews, particular objects were grouped by theme. For example, a gold elephant and gold tea set were grouped under the 'gold' case as it was also part of an enduring practice to hand gold down as dowry when a woman got married. Other central themes in the exhibition included china, textiles, educational aspirations, travel and weddings. These themes allowed the curator, Andy, to group and display particular objects in cases with an invitation to the audience to relate the experience of these families to their own personal experience.

Interview with Zahir Rafiq and Andy Pollard by Kate Pahl[9]

Kate: Zahir, can you describe your motivation in doing this project?

Zahir: As an Asian person myself, I thought it was a good idea to get positive messages across to the general public in Rotherham, to show that, you know, immigrants contribute to this town and work really hard, and to this day, the present day, they still contribute in certain ways positive images of Asians. In today's political climate, there are many stereotypes. There is a stereotype of how Asian families just think about arranged marriages. I'm not saying that doesn't go on but the majority of people are just normal, law-abiding people. I want to get across that normal view

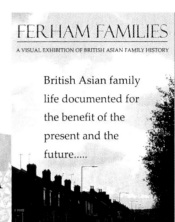

FERHAM FAMILIES
A VISUAL EXHIBITION OF BRITISH ASIAN FAMILY HISTORY

British Asian family
life documented for
the benefit of the
present and the
future.....

FERHAM FAMILIES

Every object tells a story

An exhibition celebrating the lives of Asian families living and working in Rotherham

Saturday 3rd March to Saturday 14th April 2007

Rotherham Art Gallery
Walker Place
Rotherham S65 1JH
Telephone: 01709 336633

Opening times:

Monday to Friday 9.00pm - 5.00pm
Saturday   9.00pm - 3.45pm

For more information please visit our website
www.ferhamfamilies.com

Publicity for the project by Zahir Rafiq

of Asian families, common view of Asian families, common something that the white population can relate to. Because at the moment they can't relate to Asian families, but there is so much that they can, and I hope that will come out of this project. That's why I wanted to do it, it's a great cause ... the exhibition was an opportunity to show a more detailed history of Asian families and dispel some myths and stereotypes about Asian families.

Kate: It was interesting that in the publicity for the exhibition [p. 85], the image you created was very much a 'Coronation Street' type image of the Ferham area. You also called the project 'Ferham Families'. Why was that?

Zahir: I wanted to incorporate a set of landmarks – my initial thoughts were for the people that took part. It captures their attention when they look at the poster, and it was the sense of Ferham, the area. I watch too much TV actually [laughs] and spend my time looking at soap operas and looking at people's lives – Coronation Street, Eastenders – and this gave me the idea.

Kate: How did the exhibition change people's perceptions of Asian families in Rotherham?

Zahir: In terms of the exhibition, the purpose of this project is to build a history of Asian families – there is very little out there, and if you are British Asian it is hard to just say, pick up a photo of your great-grand-dad ... is building up a history for future generations. I am interested in the commonalities, and want to get over the notion that normal Asian families 'live their lives differently'. With Ferham Families I strongly believe that it did get that message across. Take the Khan family, they were just finding work and business opportunities. For example, Mr Khan senior worked and he owned the cinema and the family contributed to the local community and they helped out a lot of other Asian families.

Kate: The exhibition had a section on gold, showing how the enduring value of gold could be seen in various ways in the families – in the decorative artefacts which showed their aesthetic interest in gold, and in the ways gold was linked to the experience of survival across the countries, and to the importance of inherited values. One of the women in the project, Ravina, described the importance of gold to us,

> As regards gold, culturally a girl is always given gold when she gets married as well as looking nice, because you wear the gold with your outfit, your wedding outfit, it is for a rainy day as well in case anything happens and you go, oh we'll sell the gold, not only are you given gold, you are given other things in the dowry, and that is like your part of your inheritance from your parents so you kind of take your inheritance with you when you get married[10]

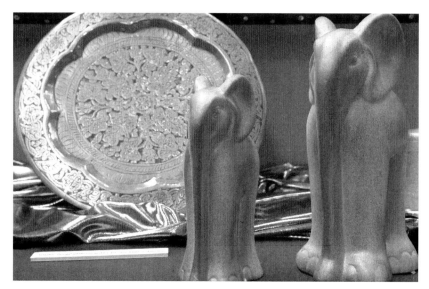

Gold case. © Steve Wright

Zahir: To me it was a heritage project – about identity – it was normalizing and bridging perceived gaps about what these people want and how they go about their lives. I think things like the children showing their favourite football team and wrestlers, the images in their bedrooms, and the stories of the uncles who worked in the Hong Kong police force, and in Britain's navy, and the armed forces were important. The family were keen to explore their New York connections, and how the great-grandfather travelled to New York – Jaan (one of the family members) was always talking about it. In terms of tracing ancestry, for Asian families how difficult would that be. Ferham families to me is the beginning of the 'who do you think you are' like the television programme [laughs].

Kate: For example, one case had a pair of shoes that related to a story about how the grandfather hid the gold that he took back from New York in his shoes. One of the family members told us that.

> The story goes that he put the money in his shoes, he had little shoes built where he could hide the gold because people would steal from you when you slept on the boat, or the train, you know, it was great difficulty, and carrying cash on you, I mean it's difficult now but in them days, he brought whatever he had back, he came all the way back to Pakistan, India, and looked after his family there.[11]

Kate: You did a lot of connecting up, people were asked to think about their own objects and family history – can you talk about that?

Shoe case. © Steve Wright

Andy: The questions that were asked in the labels – for example, what objects are precious to you? – we wanted people to interact with them. With it being themed with issues, like education, gold, it was easy to relate that to things in their own lives. The idea was to allow any visitor to relate to that and I think the visual Zahir did – of the wallpaper in the house, with things in frames [p. 89] – worked really well in connecting. It was intricately done.

Kate: The wallpaper was a photograph of the original family's front room, and on it was a designed image of key family photographs and events, as a kind of timeline of the family's history. Zahir, what did the families think of the exhibition when they came for the first time?

Zahir: On the day of the exhibition we were really stressed! Jaan was nervous. It takes a lot of courage to have your history displayed. He calmed down once he realized that the reaction from the general public was mostly positive.

Kate: Andy, what did the general public think of the exhibition?

Andy: I believe that an extremely positive picture of the local British Asian population was conveyed. There was considerable evidence presented of their experiences, hopes, and ideals. The family's contribution to the community across generations was there for all to see, as was the families' firm belief in the benefits of a good education, strong family bonds and generosity of spirit. We went in one day, and the teachers from

Wall paper by Zahir Rafiq

the local secondary school were using the space, it was their second visit, and it was a really diverse range of kids and it was really important for those families and those kids – it sent a really strong message.

The Ferham Families website

Kate: Zahir, you designed the website with the children, and devised it. Can you talk a bit about that process? One aspect you talked about at the beginning was viewing the Barbie website, which shows Barbie in her bedroom with key objects that are animated when she talks about them. You used this as an idea for the children's website, which involved screen shots of the children's bedrooms together with an image of the children's toys, with an audio-recording describing the objects – can you talk about that?

Zahir: It came quite easily. My daughter was transfixed with this Barbie website and then I thought how one could incorporate this idea into Ferham Families? I discussed it with the children, I showed them the Barbie site, the two boys said, 'Uncle' (they call me uncle) 'you can't do this'. I said, 'you can do this. You can take a picture of the bedroom at a certain angle and then take a picture of the objects and then place the objects'. They took pictures of their bedroom, and then took pictures of their favourite objects. And then, using Photoshop, I had to edit those images. By using the bedroom as background and getting individual

photos of the objects, I then cut and pasted the images on to the bedroom, making sure all those visuals are layers, like animation when you have stacks, digitally. I then transfered that on to a software called Flash. Using simple skills like photo-editing resulted in what you saw on the website.
Kate: I liked the way you used the Barbie idea, which shows Barbie in her bedroom, decorating it with chosen artefacts, as this in a way is what typifies your practice, merging different cultural concepts from Western popular culture with your own specific vision. In the children's bedrooms their objects are hybrid in the same way, from a personal copy of the Koran to a wrestling toy.

Zahir's work as an artist
Kate: Zahir, in the exhibition, your art work was also exhibited. Can you talk about your work as a contemporary Islamic artist?
Zahir: Going back to where I started – I was having coffee with a friend and he said, 'you are an artist – can you design me some Islamic art work to go with my furniture?' So I designed him a mosque and, from that, I thought, I can actually do that, and it would be a good business idea. I was on a design course at the time, and I got some sponsorship from the local college to purchase art equipment and did some paintings and got my work exhibited and I sold some more. Then I decided to make some contemporary Islamic art. People thought at that time that Islamic art was

just texts in mosques and I wanted to challenge myself and move on. I always want to gain new skills and learn different things, also as artists we have to adapt and change, and, like academics, as artists you also have to interpret the world, which is more fun. What I have learned is the importance of representing Asian families – and now I want to do this through portraits of contemporary Asian people that represent this new reality. For example, I saw a young British Asian lad the other day holding two Pit Bull terriers. I liked that. There were familiar British things when I was growing up – like riding bikes and keeping dogs – that would never have been something young British Asian people do but now they do it and it's a normal part of life in Rotherham. That to me will be one of my goals, to represent that as an artist and be part of public art work. If it wasn't for projects like Ferham Families, that kind of thing wouldn't happen. It has also given me lots of opportunities to show my other skills as a designer.

At the beginning I found it difficult to get into galleries and find spaces for my work to be shown. The major thing for me was having my first exhibition of contemporary Islamic art in a church and this provided a new vision and context for the artwork. It was also very important for me in that it had a role in educating people about Islamic faith – and after 9/11 that had more significance, and for me it was about really putting yourself out there and really sending positive messages when it was needed. I also created a multi-faith calendar for the South Yorkshire police force. What I want to do is to focus on the contemporary side, to look at British Asian families as a contemporary Islamic artist. I want to explore what is happening with Western art and mix that with Islamic art, and use mosques and textual work but in contemporary ways so that the younger generation can relate to it.

I want to do a series of portraits of contemporary Asian people. The first portrait I want to do is of my wife in a bridal gown – she has this certain expression on her face which seems to be asking what is ahead of her as a bride – there is all this build-up and discussions with parents when Asian people get married, and to have that expression, that would be my Mona Lisa. My aim is to do an exhibition of contemporary Asian lives using portraiture – I can paint and convey those complex emotions. I am always trying to challenge myself to do these kinds of things and I want to be taken seriously. It is the doing of it that is important.

Three examples of Zahir's art with explanations by Zahir Rafiq

Zahir: 'The Hope Street artwork [p. 93] was commissioned by the South Yorkshire Police Force. They wanted an image that could be put on an Eid card and be given to Mosques, Muslim organizations and local Muslim businesses. As far as I know, it was the first time that a police force had commissioned such work. The image portrays a converted mosque in a residential area with a police bicycle parked outside. By using a police bicycle, and not a motor vehicle, I hoped to portray a more sociable side of the police force. The postbox highlights that the scene is in the UK. My contact at the police force commented that the feedback from the Muslim community was really positive, and that subsequently led to a further commission from the police force to design a Multi-faith/Multicultural calendar.'

'This piece ['Cubism Allah', p. 94] puts across what I attempt to do in most of my artwork, which is to fuse Western artistic styles with traditional Islamic themes, such as text and architecture. I feel with this approach I can achieve a more contemporary look so that the artwork can appeal to Muslims who have been brought up in a Western society.'

'Most of my artistic career has focused on contemporary Islamic art, but I didn't want to be pigeon-holed. So recently I have branched out into producing portraits in oils on canvas. My first subjects were my two children. Any experienced portrait artist will tell you that painting children is notoriously difficult because you can easily paint them looking older than they are. I was quite pleased with my first attempt at portrait painting, and that gave me the confidence to go on and plan a series of paintings that reflect contemporary Asian life in Britain. Throughout my artistic career I always like to try new things and overcome challenges. I strongly believe that as an artist you should constantly strive for new goals, and hopefully this exhibition I plan to do will be an opportunity to develop my creativity further.'

Conclusion

For all of us, the project has been a journey. Andy now manages the new Claire White gallery. Kate is working on further collaborative projects with museums, and, most recently, did a digital storytelling project funded by MLA Yorkshire called 'My Family My Story', which gave families the opportunity to create their own digital stories with a local museum and a school. Zahir aims to develop his skills as an artist through his portraiture project and is involved with a public art project in the St Ann's area of Rotherham. For the families, the project provided a link to their past and

Police Eid card commission, Hope Street, *2005, medium digital.*

their heritage but also showcased valuable parts of their heritage in a public space. The families were deeply grateful for the chance to reflect on their history and to publicly celebrate their heritage. Zafran (one family member) said, this is for his children, and what greater gift can you give them than this exhibition and the website? There was a paucity of historical evidence about the family and the context for British Asian families, and this exhibition gave back some of the heritage of the area but also considered issues around the new identities of the generations growing up in Rotherham. One of the families also moved house, and the exhibition marked this move, to a new area of Rotherham. Zahir's vision as an artist held these complex in-between identities, through the images, presented in the flash presentation of objects falling through space, travelling across nations, and across neighbourhoods.

NOTES

1. For further analysis of this project, see Kate Pahl and Andy Pollard, "'Bling – the Asians Introduced that to the Country'': Gold and its Value within a Group of Families of South Asian Origin in Yorkshire', *Visual Communication* 7: 2 (2008) 170-92.
2. Interview by A.K.
3. Interview by A.K.
4. Interview by Z.K.
5. Interview by Z.K.
6. Interview by G.T.
7. Interview by Z.K.
8. Interview by Z.K.
9. Conducted on 19 July 2006.
10. Interview by R.K.
11. Interview for the project.

Cubism Allah, *2006, medium digital* [opposite]

From At the Midnight Kitchen
Mr Sufian Didan: Il-Doctoor Meets Monique

FADIA FAQIR

It was raining heavily when Sufian walked up Oxford Street. The wet paving stones shone in the artificial light of street lamps. The shop windows looked eerie in the darkness and you could only see robotic models with plastic shiny hair, some orange, others pink or purple, their lifeless large eyes gazing at you, their firm bottoms barely covered, their nippleless perky breasts pushing against flimsy fabrics. Since that incident, his wife had refused to let him touch her breasts, which was one of the punishments she dished out. It was totally out of character because Nadia was normally hanwneh: kind and compassionate. They lived in the old part of the city, where you have alleyways, balconies, lattice windows and enclosed courtyards with a fountain in the middle bubbling away. All their neighbours used to call her hanwneh. 'How is your kind wife?' they asked.

It was a hot day and he was doing a summer course at the university. He was walking hurriedly towards the campus café to meet his friend Jamil. They were going to an editorial meeting of the university newspaper. A small sweet voice coming from behind him said, 'Sir, you dropped your pen.'

He turned his head and saw a young woman, with long thick curly hair and a generous smile, pointing a pen at him. She was wearing a crisply ironed white shirt, a pair of loose blue jeans and white trainers, holding a few books and notebooks tied with a rubber band against her chest. Her clothes smelt of washing powder and her shiny black hair cascaded over slender arms. The sleeves of her long shirt were rolled up and he could see fine hairs on her arms glittering in the midday sun. He took the pen and said, 'Thank you, Miss …? Miss …?'

'Nadia,' she said, and looked down.

'Pleased to meet you.' He noticed that she was about to go. 'I'm Sufian, Miss Nadia. I'm at a loose end. Can I invite you for coffee?' He smoothed down his T-shirt.

'My next lecture begins in fifteen minutes. It's got to be quick,' she said, and lowered the books. She ran her fingers over the buttons of her shirt to make sure they had not slipped out. Suddenly he was curious about this woman standing in front of him. Why did she tilt her head sideways? Where did she live? What did she eat and drink? Was she in love, engaged, married? What was she wearing under that see-through shirt?

She looked up, then lowered her eyelashes, hiding her honey-coloured irises, and biting her lip. Sufian paled when he realized that everything had to change.

'Are you OK?' she asked.

'Yes, I'm fine. Miss Nadia, what do you study, Miss?'

'Education. I want to be a teacher. And you?'

'Media and Journalism. A journalist perhaps.' The irises of her eyes widened with approval. Warmth welled up above his stomach and under his diaphragm.

When they walked into the cafeteria he saw Jamil, in his black T-shirt and trousers, sitting at one of the tables and looking bored. He put his hand behind his back and waved Jamil off, wagging his index finger at him. He was always contrary, that bastard.

'Hello, Sufian, where have you been? I have been waiting for you for twenty minutes. Have you forgotten about our editorial meeting?' he said.

'Nadia, please meet my friend Jamil. Jamil, Miss Nadia.' Jamil shook her hand, turned round and stuck his tongue out.

'Do you like eating ma'aloubeh, Jamil? The pot is turned upside-down then kicked to loosen the risotto,' said Sufian.

'One day is for you, the next is against you,' Jamil said, and laughed.

'Exactly, my friend.' Nadia sat down, embarrassed.

Sufian looked up at the night sky and saw relentless rain coming at him through the haze of street lights. The homeless occupied every doorway of department stores where they built temporary carton shelters and left an empty plastic bowl for the loose change of passersby. Were they able to shed their families, their past or daily cares? Did they travel far from their families so they would never be found? What were their nightmares like? One of them raised his can to him and gingerly Sufian waved to him. 'You could do better,' his mother would have said. He could pack the tramp's bags, get a taxi, and take him home with him. He could give him some bread and a bowl of warm soup. He could lay a mattress for him on the sitting-room carpet and offer him a warm bed for the night. Wouldn't that be some kind of atonement?

The elegant show windows, full of plastic male models in designer suits made with fine Irish and Scottish fabrics lined the wide pavement. He used to walk in the main street with his guards, and shopkeepers bent over backwards to serve him. They offered him their merchandise for free. 'Ahlan, doctoor, welcome to my shop! You have blessed it with your presence. Here is a fine pair of trousers for your lovely figure, sidi.' Whenever he wanted a new suit he walked around the shopping centre and came back with no less than four. One day E.J. Turner, his American friend, was walking with him, the one who introduced him to the magnificent paintings of Francis Bacon. He was amazed at the reception they got. Salesgirls insisted that he took some suits as a gift from the owner. 'We will be offended if you turn us down.'

E. J. asked Sufian, 'Do you pay for all this stuff?'

Sufian ran his finger over his moustache and said, 'Yes, in kind. No, I mean in kindness,' and laughed loud.

E. J., the mighty intelligence officer, was shocked. He knew about the Arab code of 'you scratch my back and I scratch yours', but this was a step too far. 'Gee! I wish I could go to Macy's and carry all sizes of the same suit and walk out, just like that.'

'Don't worry! Those little businessmen will be asking for favours soon. A licence here, a document there, releasing goods held in the harbour, sending a brother in prison some chewing gum. That sort of shit,' he laughed.

'On their dollar, then,' E. J. smirked.

'You can't put a price on goodwill.' Sufian rubbed his index and forefinger.

Their goodwill was paramount in a country ruled by different intelligence groups, each loyal to its chief. So everyone needed protection of some sort, even the ants crawling on the ground. His came from the Big Boss himself. How many favours he owed him! 'Oh! Hello, sir! How're you? Yes, we have cleaned him up completely. Yes, room number 210, sir. Your daughter, sir, will never be harassed by him again, and can drive her car in peace. Lucky she got his number. All the streets of the capital are hers, sir. What? Yes, it is unfortunate he belongs to an outlawed political party too. Al-Qaeda? Oh yes, sir, he is al-Qaeda operative. He was also engaged in a fight before he arrived here. Not much sir, just three broken fingers, some missing toenails, and a fractured skull. He will survive, sir, but he'll not be able to turn his head while driving, and ogle at classy women. Yes, sir, he has a record now and is totally unemployable for the rest of his life. He'll beg for a crust of bread. We also confiscated his passport so he will not be able to leave this country. No, sir, he wouldn't want to leave this land of abundance. Yes, sir, the file is closed.'

In London everything was sacred: buildings, churches, vaults and towers, buses, pavements, women, and even men. So if you infringe anybody's freedom, they throw the fat book of law at you. Even the cleaner had rights and they paid her legal aid. Sufian should feel safe in such a great country, where every right was earned after blood was spilt and villages were set on fire. He knew that he was free at last. So why did he feel restless like the caged cubs on display in the president's palace gardens? But an ex-somebody like him did not deserve to be unshackled, did not deserve to walk the pavements of London and breathe fresh English air. The Big Boss treated everyone as potential traitors. 'If you don't keep a tight leash on them, they'll think they are somebody. Next thing you know they are after the food on your table.'

Sufian's office on the fifth floor of the only elegant building in the centre of the capital was modern and clean with a large glass window overlooking a busy street. Somebody – no, a 'nobody', as the boss called them – made him a cup of Arab coffee every half hour. 'Extra sugar, donkey!' he said to the veiled maid's fat hand with a cheap bulky watch, and dripped some water over the sand of his pin-cushion cactus. Affluence and power were judged by the slimness of your watch, mobile phone, computer screen, camera, tape-recorder – and the bulkiness of your files.

He looked through the window of his office and listened to the hubbub of traffic. In that godforsaken country even the clouds were subversive. They gathered surreptitiously at the end of the horizon and then suddenly your heart froze when you heard the roaring thunder. Then, before you knew it, lightning hit you, burning you down to the ground. When you least expected it, the skies opened up and poured their discontent upon your head. If the skies erupted, then it took months to clean up the rubble and debris. Yet, unlike others, he believed that cure was better than prevention. That's why they named him 'il-doctoor'. His job was to sniff the air, to measure the density of clouds, to look for ones that might turn dark and instantly liquidate them, turn them benign and harmless. It was like extracting the thorns from an erect desert cactus, then puncturing its skin with a sharp knife to spill its juices.

He sniffed the damp air of London, ran his hand over his wet hair, pulled the collar of his raincoat up, and walked on towards the park where all you needed to speak your mind was a wooden box to stand on. No public speaking for him. His secrets must remain his. Although he was a Muslim he dreamt of being a Catholic in Sicily. He would enter the dark and musty church, walk to the confessional, open the door and sit in the stall, waiting. When the curtain separating him from the screen fluttered, he would confess to the sins he had committed. He would try to convince the priest not to offer him forgiveness, but the kind, elderly padre would insist because Jesus had died to save all humanity – and particularly criminals like him. The priest would listen and then offer him words of advice, some prayer, and then absolution. He would leave the confessional and kneel down to thank God for his forgiveness. But then, suddenly, somebody would sneak up behind him and empty the five bullets of a Black Widow revolver into his head, splattering his brains on the pew and cushions.

His right shoulder was frozen, his little finger numb, and he had not eaten all day. He wiped the rain off his face with his right hand and walked on, past the shops, the fast food store, the tube station, alongside the park. In the heavy rain he could only see street lamps, car lights and the lit windows of office blocks and residential buildings. Whenever he stepped on something soft he thought it was dog shit spreading wide under the sole of his shoes. It was impure he thought and rebuked himself. He did not believe in old wives' tales, in witchcraft, magic, and nonsense. Dog shit stank, but it did not make you impure and unfit for the divine. He scraped the bottoms of his shoes against the edge of the pavement, then walked on. It was getting dark and with the rain it was hard to see what lay in front of him, but he was able to smell the fresh soil mixed with some strange chemical. Suddenly, he was about to lose his balance and keel over. His foot had slipped down a large hole dug right in the middle of the pavement. He pulled it back and steadied himself. You would think in this developed country they would put some fluorescent warning signs around the hole. But perhaps some drunken youth had removed them last night. While walking around it, he noticed the hole was full of water, which shone like a mirror and reflected the glow of buildings, the street and car lights

The smell of wet leaves, ferns, heathers and sedums, and the fetid stink of drains and gutters filled the evening air. That was London: bright blue, fuchsia, and white lights of the ice-skating and bowling hall on one side, flooded streets, the stink of gullies in the middle, and the nauseating roasted ducks dangling in the windows of restaurants on the other. He arrived in 'little Arabia', and when he walked there among the Chinese, African, Arab and Latino illegal immigrants, by shops that sold dodgy CDs, videos and computer programmes, imitation bags, and sex aids, he felt safe again. If he were to be shot it would be right here. He counted the money in his pocket, wiped his bristly upper lip where his moustache used to be, and opened the glass door of a run-down Italian cafe.

The door jingled, announcing his arrival. All eyes were on him as he stood there blinking to push the rainwater out of his eyes, his coat dripping on the tiled floor, his socks drenched and cold against his feet, his wet hair sticking to his skull. Steam rose in the middle of the café. 'Don't just stand there!' somebody shouted, in an Italian accent. 'Come in! And take off that coat before you sit on the benches!' He took off his raincoat, sat in the farthest corner, leant on the mirrored wall. When the short Italian man who shouted at him came to take the order, he said, 'Just tea and some napkins!'

He put in two spoonfuls of sugar and stirred, sipped the hot tea gingerly, put the cup down then dried his hair and face with the white napkins. It was hard sometimes. The Italian man in white shirt, black trousers, and dyed dark hair treated him with disrespect, talked to him as if he was the tea boy. In another time and place, Senor Pasta's shop window would have been smashed to smithereens in the middle of the night, his cakes flattened, his flour pissed on, his son taken to some tunnel under ground where even blue flies never flew. He cleared his throat and sipped some more tea. The liquid tingled its way down his throat, past his heart and lungs, spreading warmth and sweetness in its way. He added another spoonful of sugar, stirred, and gazed at the swirling tea. A small black fly climbed up the side of the cup, walked on the edge, and then slid down. It licked the sugar and flapped its wings until it drowned. He must will himself to live, to forgive, and look up at London and its people.

Sufian straightened his neck, pushed his jaw out, and looked at the glass storage cabinet full of biscuits, gateaux, caramel slices – and coconut tarts, his favourite. Suddenly, the door chimes jingled and she entered through the glass door. There she was: Nadia, his wife, with her curly jet-black hair and innocent eyes. Except she was younger, much younger, without strands of grey hair running down to her waist. She wore shorts that barely covered her buttocks, which protruded for all to see. He forgot about the fruit fly, drank some tea quickly, scalded his tongue and instantly spat it back into the cup. The made-up girl looked at him and smiled. Unlike his wife, whose eyes were light brown, hers were green. For a second she looked unhinged, restless like a stray dog, then her features relaxed and that savage look in her eyes was replaced with a smile. He rubbed his forehead with his good hand and smiled back.

Carrying a tray full of food, a club sandwich, fizzy drink, and espresso, she said with a French accent, '*Monsieur*, can I sit with you?' Sufian hesitated, ran his forefinger inside the collar of his shirt, listened for the sound of stray dogs, saw the embers fly out of the brazier and burn his father's fingers. He filled his nostrils with her cheap perfume, which smelt like the flowers of belladonna, with the aroma of coffee, the scent of danger. The taste of sour milk on his tongue, he said, 'Sure,' and threw his right hand in his lap so she wouldn't notice it was limp.

She put the tray on the table, took off her denim jacket and flung it on the back of the chair, separated the straps of her black shiny bra from the straps of her red top, pulled her black shorts down, pushed her hair back then sat down facing him. She held the fat sandwich in both hands, smiled, licked the sauce with her tongue, then dug her teeth into the cheese and salad stuffing. Sufian lowered his gaze. He must pay for the tea and walk out. She realized that he was about to stand, so she held his bad hand quickly, and pulled him back. How could his damaged nerves feel her softness? How could he allow anyone to touch him? He was diseased, contagious. How could he be so foolish? Sufian pulled his hand away, the same way his father used to pull his hand out of reach whenever he tried to kiss it. First, because he had so much respect for his son and did not want him to bow down to anyone, not even to his father. Then, because he was afraid of his son, of rubbing him up the wrong way. Finally, because he had nothing but contempt for him.

She said, still chewing, 'Do you have to go?' Raindrops had got everywhere, in his eyes, ears, hair, but he did not expect to see them there, gleaming in the hollow between her small breasts.

'No,' he said, and settled down.

'My name is Monique,' she said, with her mouth full.

'I am Sufian,' he said.

She puckered her glistening lips around the letters of his name, 'S-u-f-i-a-n!'

He stuck his hand in his pocket and said, 'Yes, perfect!'

'Where do you come from?' she asked.

'The Middle East. And you?'

'Me? I am French.' She pushed her curly hair away from her face. He was trained to spot lies, to see them in the angle of the finger pushing the strands of hair, in the speed of the gesture, in the length of eye contact. He knew she was lying. 'How come you're here?'

'I am a student. And you?'

'I am a businessman. Export-import, that sort of thing.'

'I see. You must be rich then,' she smiled, and ran her finger down the side of his face.

'Oh yes! Money is not the issue.' He pushed her hand away. She rubbed her knees against his under the table, lowered her cleavage, placed her arms on the table and held his elbows. The cubs in the president's palace garden were hunted down in Sudan, put in containers and flown in one of his private planes. The cages were gold-plated and they ate the finest meat every day. He lost sensation in his fingers suddenly.

'*Monsieur* Sufian, there is no harm in having some fun on such a horrible evening. *N'est-ce-pas?*' She drank some coke.

He thrust his knee between her thighs, and said, 'No.'

They walked out of the café holding hands. What if he was being filmed and all the footage was sent to his wife's work address? He would break her heart for the third time. Monique pushed her breasts against his arm and said, 'You think too much.'

He smiled, pulled her into a side street, found a dark corner by the now shut Greek shop, pushed her against the rough wall and kissed her hard on the lips. 'I want to taste your tart blood,' he said. She responded by relaxing her thighs.

'A friend of mine gave me the keys to his flat.' He was breathless now.

'Oui!' she said, nibbling at his ear.

Slices of Yorkshire:
A Short History of Sahitya Press

DEBJANI CHATTERJEE

> We are ordinary women who have written this book. But poets, prose writers and artists are not born great people; we all have the ability to create some sense of our lives on paper.[1]

It was these words, written by Safuran Ara in 1989, that inspired a group of women to establish a community publishing enterprise that is now called Sahitya Press. Conceived as a means of empowering South Asian women in South Yorkshire, the Press discovered writers who wrote mainly in Bengali. This article traces the creative trajectories of a number of these poets who took their writing seriously enough to continue with it.

Our first book was published in collaboration with the Yorkshire Art Circus (YAC) and Bengali Women's Support Group (BWSG). YAC had considerable expertise in community publishing and knew how to attract the necessary funding from Yorkshire Arts, the region's main arts funder. Earlier, in 1985, four of us had founded the Bengali Women's Support Group, a South Yorkshire community organization of predominantly Bengali-speaking Bangladeshi and Indian women. Our first anthologies – *Barbed Lines* (1990), *Sweet and Sour* (1993), *Daughters of a Riverine Land* (2003), and *A Slice of Sheffield* (2005)[2] – were Bengali-English books that were mainly written, translated, and illustrated by BWSG members. Most of the women who contributed to our anthologies initially doubted their writing abilities and asked, 'Who would want to read about us?' The material for each book was generated by holding a series of creative writing, storytelling, and visual art workshops. *Barbed Lines* and some of its successors were very much about building self-confidence. The main problem was convincing women to leave their homes and domestic chores to dedicate a few hours a month to themselves.

As Britain's first bilingual anthology in Bengali and English, *Barbed Lines* was a pioneering book in a number of respects. Produced by thirty-two members of South Yorkshire's Bengali Women's Support Group, it consisted of their stories, poems, letters and dialogues on such themes as home and identity, friendships, family, racism, education and work. In

Poetry Review, Seema Jena praised it for 'add[ing] a new dimension to Asian writing in Britain'.[3]

A notable feature of *Barbed Lines* and our subsequent anthologies is their considerable generic variety. For example, as well as devotional poetry, and autobiographical pieces about the experience of moving between different cultural domains, *Barbed Lines* also allows non-Bengali readers to discover the powerful declamatory style of Ekushey literature, that is, poems and speeches that commemorate Bengali Language Movement Day. On 21 February 1952 unarmed students in Dhaka in what was then East Pakistan were massacred for demanding the right to use Bengali as one of the state languages. Ekushey [21st] February is the anniversary of the event. Since 2000, the day has also been adopted by the UN as International Mother Language Day. The anthology, *Barbed Lines*, was published on Bengali Language Movement Day in 1990 with the stated aim of '[making] a very small contribution to keeping our language, and with it our culture and heritage, alive for ourselves and our children'.[4] Later that year, it won First Prize in the Arts Council Raymond Williams Community Publishing Competition. It sold out within the year and was reprinted in 1991. Safuran Ara and I were greatly encouraged that our small independent press had won so prestigious an award and this factor, together with the anthology's positive reception, encouraged BWSG members to produce further work with us.

Since no member of BWSG, apart from myself, had been published before, each contributor was a 'discovery'. My co-editor, Rashida Islam, was the first significant find. She had been a BWSG member for about a year when we discussed the possibility of creating *Barbed Lines*. Rashida lived in a village near Doncaster where there were no other Bengalis. A sociable woman, she felt lonely and isolated. Despite her M.Phil from the University of London, Rashida was frustrated by the lack of local job opportunities. It was Safuran, always keen to discover people's potential, who first suggested that Rashida should co-edit *Barbed Lines* with me. We ignored her protestations that she was 'a scientist, not a writer', since we had already discovered her creative streak: she loved singing and had won a prize for a science article as a college student in Dhaka. What clinched matters for us was the reluctant admission that she had kept a diary of scribbled love poems from her youth.

In our second anthology, *Sweet and Sour*, thirty women explored the importance of food in their lives: 'shopping for it, cooking, eating, feasting, fasting and dieting'.[5] In many ways, its depiction of 'Indian' food in local, domestic settings was an antidote to what Sarah Gibson refers to as British

culinary multiculturalism in this volume. As the journalist, Martin Dawes, observed in Sheffield's *The Star*: 'The recipes are interesting because they give a glimpse of the food cooked in local Asian homes which is not always the sort of thing you get in what we still call Indian restaurants.'[6] Many stories, poems, and anecdotes were accompanied with recipes, such as Tandra Chakraborty's 'Lentils Fish-head Curry'. Perhaps the most popular contribution to the book was Anima Tamuli and Raffia Mehmood's 'Handy (Alternative) Kitchen Tips', which included such rumbustious advice as

> To tenderise meat, add either green papaya, vinegar or two or three pieces of betel-nut to it during cooking. (On the other hand, you can drive the car over it two or three times before, or even after, cooking.)

and

> [D]o not throw away your vegetable peelings, they make good garden compost. (Or import a cow from India and store up good karma by feeding it.)[7]

By contrast, Maryam Khandaker Mahmud's poem, 'Food is the Centre of Life', sounded a serious note: 'Each day is a new challenge: / From where will the next meal come?'[8] *Sweet and Sour*, too, received a positive critical reception and the *Yorkshire Post* even spoke in terms of BWSG's 'quiet revolution'. Mary Sara commented,

> It will appeal to all who like to read, listen, cook and eat. Like a good meal it is a mixture of entertainment, pleasure and nourishment but it also represents something more: a reaching out to foster better cultural links from a small but talented and determined group of women.[9]

Sweet and Sour was a decisive factor in BWSG's receipt of a group award from the National Institute of Adult Continuing Education (NIACE) in 1994.

Between co-editing *Sweet and Sour* and *A Slice of Sheffield*, Rashida won a Yorkshire Arts training bursary, which enabled her to spend a year gaining experience in the independent publishing sector at Peepal Tree Press in Leeds. The bursary also enabled her to publish her own bilingual book of three stories for children, *Grandma's Treasure Trove*, in 2000.[10] Rashida had taught in Scunthorpe's primary schools, and her book began life as a resource for the children with whom she worked. Not only did she write and translate the traditional Bengali stories, she also produced the simple line-drawings that illustrated the book. At the same time she contributed an illustration to a bilingual anthology for children, *The Snake Prince and Other Folk Tales from Bengal*,[11] and wrote songs for Chol Theatre's production of a bilingual play named *Rajpathe Badshah Lear*.[12]

In Rashida's poem, entitled 'The River's Name is the Padma', Yorkshire's landscape is imaginatively overlaid with that of Bangladesh. Published in *Daughters of a Riverine Land*, the River Don in Yorkshire, which gave its name to the poet's adopted town, triggers the narrator's childhood memories of the River Padma in Bangladesh.

> For a while today, alone in the midday sun, I sat quietly
> by the River Don in the town of Doncaster
> and recalled the sweet dim memory of the Padma's past.
> Then, floating a lotus petal on the tide,
> I arrived at lost memory's gate
> to offer my heart's lotus to both the rivers.[13]

In this manner, a Sahitya Press writer transforms Yorkshire cartography.[14] Though they are continents apart, the Don mingles with the Padma in a single imagined space and the speaker's lotus petal floats on both rivers simultaneously.

A Slice of Sheffield was a very special anthology of fiction, reminiscence, poetry and artwork inspired by cutlery. It brought together the voices of over fifty women and girls from Indian, Pakistani, and Bangladeshi backgrounds in South Yorkshire. While the book recognizes Sheffield's cutlery heritage with its famous 'Made in Sheffield' stamp, it celebrates the South Asian contribution to that heritage, one that will come as a surprise to many of our readers.[15] The editorial states:

> While we wished our book to be in some sense a tribute to the proud heritage of our adopted home, we wished also to record our other legacy with its own South Asian implements and no-nonsense take on table cutlery – to share this part of our culture with others and to transmit our now dual heritage to our next generation.[16]

The book's publication by Sahitya Press, in partnership with Sheffield Galleries and Museums Trust, coincided with the Millennium Galleries' purchase of the famous Bill Brown Collection, a cutlery collection that

Cover of A Slice of Sheffield

is undeniably Eurocentric. From neolithic flint stone knives to stylish knives of stainless steel, the exhibits are all of European manufacture. Many of the items are ivory-handled, the ivory coming from India and Africa. On its part, the anthology reveals the importance of South Asian kitchen cutlery; its variety, ingenuity, and craftsmanship. It highlights 'uniquely South Asian cutlery items like *botis* or Bengali kitchen knives, *narkel kurnis* or coconut scrapers, and *jaatis* or betel nut cutters'.[17]

After viewing the Bill Brown Collection of Historic Cutlery in Sheffield's Millennium Galleries, I wrote the following clerihew for *A Slice of Sheffield*:

Bill Brown
Collector Bill Brown
admonished the Curator with a frown:
'Cutlery, Madam, is no hobby or fashion;
a political lobby, it's my life's one passion.'[18]

Our book made use of photographs from the Collection as well as from our own items of South Asian cutlery. Rashida had for long collected spoons, while I had experience of working in the steel industry in Rotherham and Sheffield, so we considered ourselves a suitable team to undertake the editing of *A Slice of Sheffield*. Apart from the book's focus on kitchen cutlery in South Asian homes, of interest to its contributors also is the South Asian reliance on eating with the fingers, as is evident from a group poem by mainly Pakistani women, 'Amma Says ...', and Gail Ranjit Pool's 'Haath Nal Khao' with its liberal sprinkling of spoken Punjabi. 'Amma Says ...' is a list poem that gives reasons for dispensing with cutlery: 'when eating *roti*, *naan* and *parathas*'.[19] Among other lovely poems in *A Slice of Sheffield* are Prema Salt's 'Ennakarandi Oil-spoon with Extended Arm', and Rashida Hassanali's tongue-in-cheek 'East and West', about 'an English teaspoon, an Indian *chamchee*'.[20] In 'Survivor of an Imperial Legacy', Yasmin Farooq views cutlery as 'a record of history':

> Sons and daughters of empire,
> we came to South Yorkshire,
> forging the steel for cutlery,
> forging the future of our 'mother country'.[21]

In 2005, *The Song of the Scythe*[22] was published in five dual language editions by Sheffield Industrial Museums Trust and Sahitya Press. I wrote it as a picture storybook about an Asian girl who visits Abbeydale Industrial Museum where she encounters the ghost of a young boy. Rashida did the Bengali translation. A year later, Sahitya Press brought out Rashida Islam's first full poetry collection, *Echoes of the Heart*, in a bilingual edition.[23] It contains a very special poem, originally written for the 'Poems for the Waiting Room' project, which is part of the charity Hyphen 21, and places poster-poems in hospitals and GPs' surgeries. It is a monologue by an unborn child in a mother's womb.

The Stranger
No moon, no stars in the deep dense dark,
what mysterious reflection wakes in me?
I am a stranger, waiting for my eyes to open,
absorbed and anxious, I have counted lonely hours
alone in my mother's womb – my own waiting room,
waiting for a zodiac sign to tell me my life's moves.

As the sunflower lifts its head for the sun to shine,
so my heart longs to see my mother's face.
Flooded by the earth's radiant light,
I will see my mother – a vision of beauty!
A growing cord of joy draws me into this world.
Within myself, I light the lamp of arrival.[24]

A co-founder of Sahitya Press, Safuran Ara also found inspiration to write through her involvement in our community publishing venture. Apart from contributing prose and poetry to *Barbed Lines*, *Sweet and Sour* and *Daughters of a Riverine Land*, she co-edited an Urdu-English oral history book, *Just for Five Years?* and, with Dolly Mondal, a Bengali poetry anthology *Kavitanjali* ('Poem Offerings').[25] Safuran and I co-edited two bilingual anthologies: an oral history book titled *Home to Home*, about the experiences of Bangladeshi women in the east end of Sheffield, and a poetry anthology, *My Birth was not in Vain*,[26] containing selections by seven of the leading contemporary women poets in Bengali from Britain, India, and Bangladesh, along with translations.

Safuran's poetry is often homely and down-to-earth. In 'Very Tasty', which appears in *Sweet and Sour*, she writes: 'Since coming to England I take new delight/ in eating arum, bitter gourds and sweet potatoes'; then goes on to describe the food she will cook for a party to be thrown for her friends, commenting that the ingredients are all 'available on Darnall's streets, /much cheaper than the market rate'.[27] In 1999, her first collection of poems, *Songs in Exile*, a bilingual book, was published by Sheffield Libraries.[28] 'Crow' is a particularly fine poem with its exposé of an ominous folk superstition and its repeated line, 'Alas, crow, you are black and hideous.'[29] 'Rickshawallah', with its delicately observed irony, is another.

A young rickshawallah
pedals with both feet
in the scorching heat of a Summer afternoon.
Sweat pours down from head to foot,
but still he pedals – faster, still faster.

Sitting behind him
are two college students, a girl and a boy.
Holding hands, they talk about
social reform and the labour movement.
The rickshawallah's heart swells to hear them.

The road's black tar is melted and sticky:
the rickshaw wheels keep stopping,
sticking in the molten tar. The rickshawallah fears
– would he manage to reach the destination?
At last, exhausted, he reaches House No. 3.

They underpay him by two takas and go inside.
Speechless, the rickshawallah breathes heavily.
They did not give his due, they were not grateful;
was this what he deserved?
And these were the very ones
who would give workers their rights![30]

Safuran's collection also includes poems about her life in Britain and,

Region / Writing / Home

specifically, Sheffield and the Gleadless estate where she lived. All her poems are characterized by their ready accessibility. My translation of Safuran's feminist poem, 'A Bengali Woman in Britain', originally published in Bengali in *Kavitanjali*, appeared in the *Guardian* on National Poetry Day, 9 October 2003.

A Bengali Woman in Britain

A Bengali woman in Britain earns her bread,
her life is not confined by narrow limits.
Hard looks can hold no threat for her,
she is no homeless victim or beggar.

A Bengali woman in Britain does not easily surrender.
She is no still and silent statue.
Nothing startles her, no sudden noise;
she is no golden deer caught in a veil of illusion.

Though far from home, she is no straw adrift on the tide.
The scent of lemon, moonlight dancing on tamarind leaves,
music in the drizzling of Monsoon nights, grip her in nostalgia.
Even today such sweet memories have not dimmed.

A Bengali woman in Britain
has yearnings unfulfilled but her head is unbowed.
She is no wretch to crawl in anyone's dust.
Do not view her with pity, she is no beggar.

A Bengali woman in Britain
arose one dawn and flew, she soared wild on wings.
She is not insignificant, she needs no looks of sympathy,
she is no angelic being, nor some drunkard's slut.
She is no mysterious goddess, she wants no worship.[31]

On the surface, Safuran's poem would seem to echo Rehana Chaudhury's 'We are the Women of Bengal' from *Barbed Lines*. But Rehana's poem glorifies what are considered essentially 'feminine' virtues:

We are the women of Bengal –
our patience like the tolerant earth's.
We contain all pain within ourselves
to create peace for others.[32]

Safuran's Bengali woman, on the other hand, is, like its author, bold and assertive, a woman of flesh and blood. As its name might suggest, *Songs in Exile*, is suffused with longing for the motherland that has been left behind. 'A Bengali Woman in Britain' is lyrical on this subject, while, in 'Friend', Safuran writes of her 'despair / in this foreign land of satanic industry', until a surprise meeting with a friend reinvigorates hope through memories of how 'our common soil bound our hearts as one, my friend and I'.[33]

After living in South Yorkshire for most of her adult life, Safuran returned to resettle in Bangladesh at the end of 2003. Her departure was perhaps precipitated by a nervous breakdown in 1999. 'Sheffield is a great place,' she told her friends, 'but this is no country to live in if you are old and single.' The sixth Sahitya Press anthology, *Daughters of a Riverine Land*, is dedicated to Safuran Ara and, as a parting gift, the Bengali Women's Support Group awarded her honorary Life Membership. She now lives in Dhaka with an adopted son and daughter-in-law, runs the Desh School for slum children, and occasionally revisits Sheffield.

Chesterfield-based Ashoka Sen co-edited *Daughters of a Riverine Land* with me. A bilingual writer and visual artist, she returned to her studies after her widowhood and, among other successes, achieved an MA in Creative Writing from Sheffield Hallam University. I anthologized two of her poems in *The Redbeck Anthology of British South Asian Poetry*. 'The Past like the Chorus Character' begins:

> When all the voices outside go quiet at night,
> the past rises.
> Like the chorus character of a Greek play,
> it starts telling and interpreting the events
> of our yesterday,
> linking them to the present.[34]

Eight years later, her first picture storybook, *An Untouchable King*, was published by AuthorHouse.[35]

Rotherham-based Dolly Mondal was another writer who co-edited an anthology for us. She joined Safuran Ara in editing *Kavitanjali* and contributed fine poems to the Bengali anthology as well as to *Barbed Lines* and *Sweet and Sour*. Her 'Seasonal Gifts' in *Sweet and Sour* is a sensuous celebratory poem:

> An abundance of juicy mangoes
> marinates the Summer's heat
> and the season's precious showers
> bring floods of star-apples to the bough.
> As Autumn dawns the soil is sanctified
> with shoots of rice and our hearts overflow.
> The earth fills with golden growth,
> swaying gently as the evenings mellow.
> With Winter's gift of newly ripened rice,
> housewives, with gracious hands, prepare
> the feast that lightens each Bengali heart.

Spring splashes Holi colours everywhere,
Palash trees burst with flaming splendour
and romance blossoms between man and wife.[36]

Daughters of a Riverine Land contains Mina Begum's charming 'journey'
poem, 'From Sylhet to Sheffield'.

My village in Sylhet has many streams.
Small and friendly, they invited our play;
each day after school I'd go with my friends,
we'd splash in the waters and sing and shout.
I thought this life would go on forever.

Then my family flew across the seas.
Everything was strange in a foreign land:
the language, the food, the weather, the school.
My world was upside down and I'd rush home
each day after school. I longed to fly back.

Sheffield was so large – I longed to escape
but its small and friendly streams spoke of home.
With my sisters and brothers I grew up
in this city, learnt English and made friends.
Now our children play beside the canal.[37]

In noting the poetry of South Asian women whose talent has been
nurtured by Sahitya Press, I should not omit my own work as a poet. I had
been writing poetry for many years before the Press was founded and my
first full collection *I Was that Woman* was launched at Sheffield's first Off-
the-Shelf Literature Festival in 1989.[38] My involvement in Sahitya Press
and, later, in the writers' group called Mini Mushaira, undoubtedly
contributed to my development as a poet. It was also largely responsible
for encouraging me to become a literary translator.

Barbed Lines takes its title from a line in my Peterloo Prize-winning
poem called 'To the English Language'. The poem charts a journey to a
language, a country, and a culture. In the process, it describes a poet's
development:

To the English Language
Indifferent language of an alien shore,
the journey was troubled but I am here:
register me among your step-children.

That special love that flows easy with my birthright
is for Bengali, my mother – a well rounded tongue,
sweet and juicy with monsoon warmth,
rich and spicy with ancestral outpourings.

What has proficiency to do with it?
I know I dream it endlessly.

English, your whiplash of thoughts
has scarred me, pebbles rattle in my mouth
while innuendoes turn my tongue.

For generations you called to me,
siren of the seven western seas,
though now you may deny this and tell me
to go back where I came from.
Your images were the barbed lines
that drew me, torn, to this island keep.

Your words raise spectral songs to haunt me.
I have subverted your vocabulary
and mined rebellious corridors of sound.
I have tilled the frozen soil of your grammar
– I will reap the romance of your promises.

I know you now
with the persistence that a stranger musters.
I know the madness hidden in your rules and relics,
I see the glory where you would disown it.
I know my own desperate yearning,
but I do not come to your rhythms empty-handed
– the treasures of other traditions are mine,
so many koh-i-noors, to be claimed.

It is now my turn to call you at my homecoming.
I have learnt to love you
– the hard way.[39]

The anthology *Daughters of a Riverine Land* included the experimental
ghazal, 'An "Indian Summer"', which connects the River Mandakini in
Heaven, the River Ganges in India, and the canal in Sheffield:

September – and I see the urban fisher-folk
dreaming of salmon leaping in roaring rivers.

Sunday in Sheffield – and I walk by the canal.
The high Himalayas drum with roaring rivers.

The dragonfly flits in the Yorkshire afternoon
while Mandakini descends in roaring waters.

Once a laughing goddess roamed along these banks;
now unknown, her name resounds through roaring waters.

Ducks swim, ruffling their feathers over this landscape.
Yards away, industry storms its roaring waters.

Whatever she is called, Ganga meditates
on Summer rippling the calm of English rivers.[40]

Traditionally, ghazals carry no titles and the poet's name is inserted in a final 'signature' couplet. But, with a few notable exceptions, I like my poems to have titles and generally give my ghazals titles too. In 'An "Indian Summer"' I have not inserted my name in the final couplet but, as a compromise, I have included the name Ganga to indicate both the Goddess and the river. Rather than rigidly maintain a refrain at the end of each couplet, as the true ghazal requires, I have slightly varied the refrain by using two versions of it in alternate verses.

Poems that adhere more strictly to the form also appear in my writing from time to time. Thus, 'Theatre', which is in my most recent collection *Words Spit and Splinter* and describes a traumatic episode at Sheffield's Northern General Hospital, keeps faith with the ghazal form:

Theatre
(For Jan Wilson for her support following a traumatic experience at Northern General Hospital)

The world somersaults, forsaking control.
Dizzy, freefalling, forsaking control.

Trapped in a bubble, fists pound against walls.
No brakes, no steering, forsaking control.

Gloved and masked, the torturers are in charge.
Silently screaming, forsaking control.

Flesh is stretched and severed, skewered and stitched.
On pain waves floating, forsaking control.

The world's oppression weighs down on the chest,
Life-blood escaping, forsaking control.

A tangle of hushed voices surround her;
Debjani is resisting forsaking control.[41]

'An "Indian Summer"' had reminded the reader that, like the Ganges, many English rivers too, including those of Sheffield, were worshipped in pre-Christian times. A few stanzas from a much longer poem, 'For No Soul Should Linger …', first broadcast by the BBC, also have the River Soar near Loughborough shading into the Ganges and the Baitaruni, the mythological river of the underworld:

Like every river in every land, the Soar
is a new Baitaruni, an English Lethe,
transporting souls to the *shanti* of *moksha*.

....

Our boat stops below a motorway bridge
where eddies of water swirl as if welcoming
Excalibur or the rising of Goddess Ganga.

....

The splendid audacity of Bhagirath's prayers
brought Heaven's own river Mandakini tumbling
over Shiva's locks, and washing ancestral ashes.

Bhagirath's children in Vilayat today,
we too have brought the Ganges here;
across seven seas and thirteen rivers we have come.

Our bodies die, but the soul lives on;
our rivers change, but the Ganges is everywhere.
We pour its water in the twice-blessed Soar!

As Heaven's river Mandakini became Ganga,
India's sacred river is now the English Soar.
Shiva embraces her in all our million locks.[42]

'More Than I Wear' was written as a tribute to a group of South Asian
teenage girls in Halifax who had put together their own idiosyncratic
clothes exhibition:

More Than I Wear
(for the young women in the Asian Women's Resource Association)

A young woman, Asian and British,
I have swallowed the world's rough oyster
  – pearl and all; yes, pearl and all.

I've had hard times and will face worse times,
but my gear is sorted and, sister,
    right now, I'm having a ball!

I move to Indi-pop and bhangra,
dupatta flying from my shoulder
    – angel wings and waterfall.

    The world is my oyster – pearl and all.
    Sister, right now, I'm having a ball!

Dadiji gave me this hand-stitched *chunni*.
Her love flows through it like a river,
   and I float tall – I float tall.

    The world is my oyster – pearl and all.
    Sister, right now, I'm having a ball!

I bought myself this denim jacket
and embroidered a lotus flower
   – there's none like it in the mall!

    The world is my oyster – pearl and all.
    Sister, right now, I'm having a ball!

My silk *kameez* glows with gold sequins
my satin *salwar* mirrors the hour
   in Halifax and Bengal.

    The world is my oyster – pearl and all.
    Sister, right now, I'm having a ball!

My Doc Martens pack a feisty kick.
I am from Bradford and Jullunder,
   Mirpur, Punjab and Walsall.

    The world is my oyster – pearl and all.
    Sister, right now, I'm having a ball!

I'm more than I wear: Asian British.
My clothes are those that eye the future,
with respect for tradition's power.
Sari or jeans, I am the daughter
   of Birmingham and Southall.

    The world is my oyster – pearl and all.
    Sister, right now, I'm having a ball!
    Sister, right now, I'm having a ball![43]

In conclusion and, as a vision for future generations, let me offer an extract from 'Mothers and Daughters', a group poem created with some women at Roshni Asian Women's Resource Centre. The togetherness that it celebrates is not merely a family relationship, but also a metaphor for the blending of cultures that is taking place in our region:

Mothers and daughters,
   together
like fish and chips,
like salt and pepper,
like idli and dhosa,

like kulfi and pesta badaam,
like aloo and gobi,
like daal and rice,
like spinach and roti,
like bread and butter,
like custard and pudding,
like coffee and cream,
like crackers and cheese,
like milk and *rasamalai* –
just right together.[44]

NOTES

1. Safuran Ara, 'Bengali Women's Support Group' in *Barbed Lines*, eds, Debjani Chatterjee and Rashida Islam (Sheffield and Castleford: Bengali Women's Support Group and Yorkshire Art Circus, 1990), p. 16. Trans. Safuran Ara and Debjani Chatterjee.
2. Debjani Chatterjee et al, eds, *Sweet and Sour* (Sheffield: Bengali Women's Support Group, 1993); Debjani Chatterjee & Ashoka Sen, eds, *Daughters of a Riverine Land* trans. Debjani Chatterjee (Sheffield: Bengali Women's Support Group, 2003); Debjani Chatterjee and Rashida Islam, eds, *A Slice of Sheffield* (Sheffield: Sahitya Press and Sheffield Galleries and Museums Trust, 2005).
3. Seema Jena, 'Review of *Barbed Lines*', *Poetry Review* 83:1 (1993) 24.
4. Chatterjee and Islam, 'To the Reader', *Barbed Lines*, p. 10.
5. Chatterjee et al, *Sweet and Sour*, p. 10.
6. Martin Dawes, *The Star*, 18 September 1993.
7. Anima Tamuli and Raffia Mehmood, 'Handy (Alternative) Kitchen Tips', in *Sweet and Sour*, trans. Ruma Tamuli, pp. 141-42.
8. Maryam Khandaker Mahmud, 'Food is the Centre of Life', in *Sweet and Sour*, p. 124.
9. Mary Sara, 'A Sweet and Sour View of Cooking', *Yorkshire Post*, 8 September 1993.
10. Rashida Islam, *Grandma's Treasure Trove* (Sheffield: Bengali Women's Support Group, 2000). Bilingual book with translations by the author.
11. Debjani Chatterjee and Rehana Chaudhury, eds, *The Snake Prince and Other Folk Tales from Bengal* (Sheffield: Bengali Women's Support Group, 1999).
12. Produced in 1998, this play was a multilingual (English-Urdu-Bengali) play, which can be translated as 'King Lear on the Street'. This version of the King Lear story offers its own transcultural comment on rural and urban tensions.
13. Rashida Islam, 'The River's Name is the Padma', in *Daughters of a Riverine Land*.
14. For an interesting discussion of alternative cartographies of migration, see Roger Rouse, 'Mexican Migration and the Social Space of Postmodernism', *Diaspora*, 1: 1 (1991) 8–23.
15. See Nima Poovaya-Smith, 'Review', in *Performing Arts and South Asian Literature*, *Moving Worlds*, 5:2 (2005) 147-48.
16. Chatterjee and Islam, eds, 'Editorial', in *A Slice of Sheffield*, p. 13.
17. Chatterjee and Islam, eds, 'Editorial', in *A Slice of Sheffield*, pp. 11-13.
18. Chatterjee and Islam, eds, *A Slice of Sheffield*, p. 25.
19. Chatterjee and Islam, eds, *A Slice of Sheffield*, p. 69.
20. Rashida Hassanali, 'East and West', in *A Slice of Sheffield*, p. 37.
21. Yasmin Farooq, 'Survivor of an Imperial Legacy', in *A Slice of Sheffield*, p. 61.
22. Debjani Chatterjee, *The Song of the Scythe* (Sheffield: Sahitya Press and Sheffield Industrial Museums Trust, 2005).

23. Rashida Islam, *Echoes of the Heart,* trans., Debjani Chatterjee (Sheffield: Sahitya Press, 2006).
24. Islam, *Echoes of the Heart,* p. 7.
25. Mohammed Iqbal, Safuran Ara and Rachel Van Riel, eds, *Just for Five Years? Reminiscences of Pakistani Senior Citizens in Sheffield* (Sheffield: Sheffield City Libraries, 1990); Safuran Ara and Dolly Mondal, eds, *Kavitanjali* (Sheffield: Bengali Women's Support Group, 1994).
26. Debjani Chatterjee and Safuran Ara, eds, *Home to Home,* trans. Debjani Chatterjee (Sheffield: Sheffield Libraries, 1995), Debjani Chatterjee and Safuran Ara, eds, *My Birth was not in Vain: Selected Poems by Seven Bengali Women* (Sheffield: Sheffield Libraries, 2001).
27. Safuran Ara, 'Very Tasty', in *Sweet and Sour*, trans. Sabira Azad, p. 73.
28. Safuran Ara, *Songs in Exile,* trans. Debjani Chatterjee (Sheffield: Sheffield Libraries, 1999).
29. Safuran Ara, 'Crow', in *Songs in Exile,* p. 60.
30. Safuran Ara, 'Rickshawallah', in *Songs in Exile,* , p. 65.
31. Safuran Ara, 'Bengali Woman in Britain', in *Songs in Exile,* , p. 57.
32. Rehana Chaudhury, 'We are the Women of Bengal', trans. Rehana Chaudhury and Debjani Chatterjee, in *Barbed Lines*, p. 16.
33. Safuran Ara, 'Friend', in *Songs in Exile,* p. 71.
34. Ashoka Sen, 'The Past like the Chorus Character', in *The Redbeck Anthology of British South Asian Poetry*, ed., Debjani Chatterjee (Bradford: Redbeck Press, 2000), p. 135.
35. Ashoka Sen, *An Untouchable King – An Indian Folk Tale* (Milton Keynes: AuthorHouse, 2008).
36. Dolly Mondal, 'Seasonal Gifts', trans., Dolly Mondal and Debjani Chatterjee, in *Sweet and Sour*, p. 90.
37 Mina Begum, 'From Sylhet to Sheffield', in *Daughters of a Riverine Land*, p. 67.
38. Debjani Chatterjee, *I Was that Woman* (Frome: Hippopotamus Press, 1989).
39. Chatterjee, 'To the English Language', in *I Was that Woman,* p. 27.
40. Debjani Chatterjee, 'An "Indian Summer"', in *Namaskar: New and Selected Poems*, ed., Debjani Chatterjee (Bradford: Redbeck Press, 2004), p. 118.
41. Debjani Chatterjee, *Words Spit and Splinter* (Bradford: Redbeck Press, 2009), p. 46.
42. Chatterjee, 'For No Soul Should Linger ...' in *Words Spit and Splinter*, pp. 19-21.
43. Chatterjee, 'More than I Wear', in *Namaskar: New and Selected Poems*, pp. 136-37.
44. Members of Sheffield Roshni Asian Women's Resource Centre, 'Mothers and Daughters' in *A Slice of Sheffield*, p. 97.

Basir Sultan Kazmi – An Introduction

I am a Manchester-based writer working in traditional eastern forms. The ghazal is an established and extremely popular verse-form in Urdu and Persian. It is a traditional type of short lyric poem that can be recited, chanted, and sung, with or without musical accompaniment. While the ghazal can cover any topic, love has always been its pre-eminent subject. The thoughts expressed in ghazals are usually not tied to any particular locale but sometimes an odd couplet betrays the location that the poet had in mind while composing it. For example, two of my couplets, from different ghazals, clearly hint at displacement. The literal translation of these is:

> I, who had regarded every piece of cloud as a blessing
> Came to this city and yearned for sunshine

> I wouldn't have missed my city that much
> But I can't help it as your city's weather is rough

Intizar Hussein, the distinguished Urdu fiction writer and critic, has highlighted this aspect in his review of my latest collection of poetry.

> His familiarity and friendship with poets from different cultures and languages has paid him well. In fact, the verses in this collection tell the tale of a long drawn out conflict and eventual reconciliation with the land he has chosen to live in. – This tells us about the change in his poetic experience, which was brought about by his migration to a foreign land. – So we see this poet growing in a western land while exposed to inter-cultural influences. – Among the blessings he has lost because of migration is sunshine. And sunshine is among those precious things he yearns for. ('Dawn', Lahore, 25 January 2009)

Like the sonnet, the ghazal has strict requirements of structure, content and imagery. It uses a single uniform metre in every line – and often a very complex metrical pattern is used, as well as a rhyming scheme of AA, BA, CA, DA, and so on. Each individual couplet of a ghazal is a complete and autonomous entity, and frequently differs from the adjoining couplets in theme and mood. But there is an overall unity in the shape of the poem, the metre and the patterning of language and images. Themes can also recur in the same ghazal. In the final couplet, in most cases, the poet introduces his or her own name, or penname.

BASIR SULTAN KAZMI

Ghazals

TRANSLATED FROM URDU INTO ENGLISH BY THE AUTHOR AND DEBJANI CHATTERJEE

1. Finding One's Place

Everyone settles at last, each in their own place.
No one can stay for long in someone else's place.

Everyone must find and build a place of their own,
even if it seems they have a ready-made place.

Where all are content in their own respective space –
in my imagination there *is* such a place.

There is no charm here in living, or in dying.
Who counselled you to inhabit another's place?

I grumble about you, but there is also love.
There is room for both – each has its distinctive place.

That site of which you have been neglectful, Basir –
that is none other than *your* own space, your true place.

Note: Qais or Majnoon was the legendary star-crossed lover of Leila.

2. The True-Hearted

The true-hearted can settle – no matter which land.
A flower wants to bloom, wherever its garden.

If the gossip must be about current affairs,
then anyone may be engaged – in any crowd.

The same lack of reward awaits accomplished hands.
In the end the mountain-cutter breaks his own head.

Those who are ambitious do not depend on wine;
day or night, they stay drunk, whatever their longing.

I await the art-lover as I would some dear one.
I spread eyes and heart in their path, whoever they are.

When do habits and desires ever change, Basir?
Whichever the forest, a peacock needs must dance.

Note: Shireen's lover Farhad broke his head when he could not win his beloved even
after he had fulfilled the difficult task of cutting a stream of milk through the mountain.

3. Tomorrow's Trees

Those tender shoots, crushed by the hurricane at dawn,
held tomorrow's trees, bushy with leaves and blossom.

In search of new companions I forsook your friendship
and left your city, but nowhere could I meet your equal.

The same customary coldness is here, the same dark night.
What is the point of burning here, O lamps of my city?

I chase new dreams; my seashore lies under water.
What will you gain, my friends, by walking by my side?

In this half-ravaged house, in this flickering heart,
here in this very heart – too many suns have set.

Now through the evening hours someone speaks to my heart:
'Some moon should surely rise, some cup should overflow.'

This is what I have observed in my life's journey, Basir:
those who tread with greatest caution are the ones who stumble.

4. Passing Through

Even if she lives here, I can never hope to meet her.
Wherever she may live, her happiness is my prayer.

O my desolate heart, what a strange wish is this of yours:
to want her to show herself at once cruel and tender.

Paradise has not yet been created on Earth, my friends.
The place of which you speak – know that I too have lived there.

My bags have always been few and my luggage weighed little.
Like a nomad just passing through, I have lived here and there.

Basir, even those unworthy of making the journey,
became leaders of the caravan, leading it nowhere.

5. Pledge

The atmosphere of days gone by comes to the mind.
That moonlight, that house, that breeze – they enter the mind.

It is as if someone somewhere is calling me.
At midnight, whose voice is this that enters the mind?

I sought no cure when separation's wound was fresh;
now incurable, remedies enter the mind.

Even though it's distant, that face is so gracious:
when remembered by the heart, it enters the mind.

Today, Basir was to pledge himself to someone,
when suddenly another's pledge entered the mind.

6. Your Arrows Of Memory

How could I sing so sweetly in times so bitter?
Don't ask how I managed to orchestrate my tongue.

All those who are displaced because of your neglect –
say, how may they now be restored? Pray, tell me how?

Your arrows of memory perforate my heart.
How will this sieve contain the melancholic storm?

The breeze of poetry revives my life's garden:
how every branch and every single petal sways.

A beauty has come to live in my heart's abode.
How can I make her vacate it, I now wonder.

It takes a long time, Basir, to achieve patience.
How did you earn this wealth in the course of one day?

Questioning Black Identity: Strategies of Digression in E.A. Markham's *Meet Me in Mozambique*

LUCY EVANS

E.A. Markham's short story, 'Seminar on the Frank Worrell Roundabout, Barbados', takes place in a taxi where a creative writer due to speak at a conference prevaricates by directing the driver to stay on the roundabout rather than turn off up the road to the university. Hints as to the reason behind her hesitancy emerge during the course of the narrative. The writer, named Eye See Eye, silently challenges the taxi driver's presumed prejudices by reflecting that 'in England she is written up as a West Indian writer, whatever her colour, and she can buss bad word with the rest of them'.[1] This detail, along with her half-formed plan to arrive at the conference carrying 'a copy of Kamau Brathwaite's *Barbajan Poems* to deflect attention',[2] implies that Eye See Eye is a white writer masquerading as African Caribbean. Indeed, the name 'Eye See Eye' indicates a shift from an eye to eye connection between writer and readers to a more oblique relationship. The approach of a writer who presents herself indirectly to readers is expressed visually in her protracted journey on the roundabout with its several possible exits. In his collection of interlinked stories, *Meet Me in Mozambique*,[3] Markham's narrative strategies are similarly circuitous. He invents three fictional versions of himself in the figures of Pewter Stapleton, Michael Carrington, and Colin Retford, cast in some stories as narrators and in others as protagonists, and always intent on 'sending [each other] up' (p. 88). This article will explore how this mode of parodic self-writing offers Markham a means of commenting critically upon the role ascribed to him by British critics and cultural organizations as a black writer. In presenting himself in a roundabout way, I will argue, Markham examines his own public image, and in doing so raises broader questions regarding the marketing and reception of black British writers. I am concerned with the ways in which strategies of digression, operating both in the text's structure and narrative mode, enable Markham to interrogate constructions of black identity from the postwar period into the twenty-first century.

In *Against the Grain: A 1950s Memoir*, Markham tells of his attempts to become a playwright in the 1950s and 1960s. He picks out the example of a play set in West London, in which BBC Radio Wales had expressed an interest:

> I was surprised that their main recommendation for revision was to make more of the Notting Hill riots of a few years back. I was wary about being labelled as someone who wrote about 'black' or 'race' issues (and to being told what a 'black issue' was). Whatever the reason, maybe a bit of intransigence on my side, the play was never broadcast.[4]

Later in the memoir, Markham remarks how 'the ethnicizing of Caribbean/West Indian into "black" has happened', and, as a result, 'attempts to define "black" arts (now as a political colour, now as a way of facilitating inclusion; again as a way of asserting separateness)' have been 'a feature of the last few decades'.[5] Markham's resistance to the category 'black' in the 1950s and 1960s, seen in his earlier refusal to revise his play, prefigured the thinking of writers, artists, literary critics and cultural theorists on this subject in subsequent decades. His comment on 'attempts to define "black" arts' acknowledges this, offering a concise summary of changing approaches to black identity in the period 1970s to the 1990s.

With his reference to the use of the term 'black' as a 'political colour', Markham alludes to what Alison Donnell describes as the 'politicisation of black consciousness in the 1970s', where the articulation of black identity served as a 'vital, if limited, platform for self-representation' in a situation where migrants of African, Caribbean, and South Asian descent were subjected to 'state racism'.[6] Equally, the idea of 'black' 'as a way of facilitating inclusion' relates to Donnell's identification of a movement in the 1980s away from a concern with political solidarity within the migrant community towards a recognition of internal differences, as black cultural production 'began to reflect the need to articulate the multiple imbrications of identity'.[7] Finally, 'black' as 'a way of asserting separateness' could be seen as an observation of the shift in the 1990s away from 'collective definition' against a hostile white 'host culture' and towards 'complex and diverse acts of self-definition' in the context of a growing multiculturalism.[8] Markham's interrogation of black identity thus begins with the racial stereotyping he encountered in the 1950s as part of the *Windrush* generation, and extends through several decades of black cultural production. His criticisms of a predominantly white postwar British society must therefore be analysed alongside his scepticism towards the way in which the concept of blackness has been deployed by writers, cultural organizations, and critics in the second half of the twentieth century. Both in his memoir and in his fictional writing, Markham implies that the constraints placed upon writers by the category 'black' have not dissolved over time, but rather have operated in different ways with each stage in the development of a black British literary tradition.

In his influential essay, 'Black Art and the Burden of Representation', Kobena Mercer describes how black artists have been 'burdened with the impossible task of speaking as "representatives," in that they are widely expected to "speak for" the marginalized communities from which they come'.[9] Quoting Paul Gilroy, Mercer considers how this has imposed upon black artists 'a set of ethical "obligations"' which renders them 'accountable to' their communities in their aesthetic choices.[10] He places in question this notion of the black artist's social responsibility with his later reference to 'the violence entailed in speaking *for* others'.[11] In this light, to decline a representative role would seem the more ethical path to take. The ideas expressed in Mercer's essay overlap with some of the central concerns of Markham's writing. In his essay 'Roots and Roots' (2003), Markham explores the dangers of seeing the migrant community portrayed by Sam Selvon in his 1956 novel *The Lonely Londoners* as representative of the *Windrush* generation. He claims that 'no Caribbean person reading *The Lonely Londoners* at the time would have taken this *accurate* portrait of youngish, mainly male, good-humoured and resilient migrants … as a cross-section of Caribbean … society'.[12] While he does not doubt the 'accuracy' of what Selvon's has depicted of postwar London, he stresses the need to recognize it as partial.

With his recurring trope of the transported drawing room – introduced in an earlier volume of short stories, *Taking the Drawing Room Through Customs* (2002), and reappearing in both the *Meet Me in Mozambique* collection and the memoir – Markham complements Selvon's primarily male and working-class migrant community with the middle-class consciousness of a family which has left behind a twelve-roomed house complete with servants on arrival in London in the mid-1950s.[13] In *Meet Me in Mozambique*, the semi-autobiographical Pewter Stapleton repeatedly insists upon the social and cultural specificity of his family's experiences. For example, in the story 'The Mosley Connection', he reflects upon his family's position as a 'special case', since 'we never quite saw ourselves as a migrant family' (p. 96). He goes on to provide an extensive list of justifications for this statement: his family is 'middle-class', with a 'status' that they expect to be 'recognized in England'; they are from a British colony rather than an independent Caribbean island, so are in effect British citizens; there is a history of family members going to war for England; and, crucially, they 'did not *have* to come to England' (p. 97).

If Markham's precise and thorough portraiture of his family allows him to challenge homogenizing applications of the term 'black', the digressive structure of *Meet Me in Mozambique* provides him with a way of confronting nationally bounded narratives of black British literary history. In 'Seminar on the Frank Worrell Roundabout, Barbados', Markham presents readers with 'the idea of a roundabout to solve your problems of space'; a roundabout's multiple turn-offs, he proposes, give small island inhabitants a sense of 'possibilities' and of 'not being hemmed in'.[14] In a similar way, I suggest, the meandering journeys of Markham's narrators and protagonists in *Meet Me in Mozambique* serve to expand the imaginative geography of black Britain. In 'Fantasy Relationships: Black British Canons in a Transnational World', John McLeod points out that in 'privileging the national', many black British anthologies have sidelined 'a number of transnational and translational circuits and axes'.[15] As a result, he explains, 'literary tradition becomes spatially constricted'.[16] As is indicated by its title, *Meet Me in Mozambique* foregrounds international travel, and thus works against the narrowing process identified by McLeod.

Yet Markham's short story collection sits uneasily with even those theories of black identity which accentuate the transnational. Written and partially set in Sheffield, *Meet Me in Mozambique* moves between several continents, mirroring the globetrotting existence of the characters within it. The volume consists of fifteen stories, divided into two parts entitled 'The St. Caesare Connection' and 'The Mozambique Connection'. These subheadings might at first glance appear to organize the material; it seems appropriate that the first section would deal with Markham's Caribbean childhood, since St. Caesare is a fictional version of the author's native Montserrat, and that the second section would address his ancestral heritage, since Mozambique is an African country. However, on closer inspection, it becomes evident that the book's content defies this logic. The first part does indeed include stories set in St. Caesare which feature both a younger Pewter living with his grandmother in the Stapleton estate house, and an older Pewter returning temporarily to the island after an extended period abroad. Nevertheless, the positioning of these stories among others set in London, Manchester, Sheffield, Budapest, Uganda and China de-emphasizes the significance of the Caribbean as a cultural marker in Markham's self-writing process. The second section seems to be arranged in an equally haphazard manner. 'On the Game' takes place in Sheffield, and 'Notes at Maputo Airport' occurs mainly in transit between countries. The misleadingly named 'The Dakota Club' combines the settings of Sheffield and Mozambique; and the title story, 'Meet me in Mozambique', strays between St. Caesare, Luton, Manchester, Paris, the South of France, London, Doncaster and Sheffield before finally reaching the country mentioned in its title. Moreover, the spatial coordinates of the last three stories increasingly recede as Pewter's invented alter-ego Colin Retford negotiates Pewter's fictional universe, and as Pewter subsequently enters it himself in order to 'track down Colin Retford' (p. 242).

The subheadings' promise of meaningful 'connections' between places and times in Markham's life experience and family history is therefore undermined as we progress through the stories, resulting in a reading experience comparable to the delayed and diverted train and aeroplane journeys featured within the text.[17] The thematic and formal wanderings of *Meet Me in Mozambique* complicate Paul Gilroy's conceptual mapping of a black Atlantic consciousness in relation to the 'triangular' compass of the slave trade.[18] Gilroy bases his cultural analysis mainly on the United States and Britain, with passing references to the Caribbean and Africa. In Markham's stories, however, Britain becomes just one location in a range of European settings. Furthermore, whereas Gilroy discusses parts of Africa connected with transatlantic slavery, such as Liberia and Sierra Leone, *Meet Me in Mozambique* features African countries which fall outside the history of slavery. Pewter's comment in 'Notes at Maputo Airport' offers an insight into the reasons behind Markham's choice of Mozambique as a final destination for his three alter-egos: he confides that 'one of the reasons Mozambique appealed' to him was that it involved 'no tracing of West African slave routes' (p. 169). The seemingly disorganized structure of *Meet Me in Mozambique* could, then, be read as strategic in its resistance to a black Atlantic mapping.

Equally, both the routes taken and the characters' manner of travelling unsettle the notion of constitutive journeys put forward in Stuart Hall's 'Cultural Identity and Diaspora'. Hall acknowledges that Africa 'cannot in any simple sense be merely recovered' by African Caribbean people, and that a journey 'home' to Africa is therefore impossible. Nevertheless, he stresses the importance of Africa as 'a necessary part of the Caribbean imaginary', arguing that 'symbolic journeys' back to an imagined Africa are a means by which new cultural identities have been developed. This 'displaced "homeward" journey' is 'necessarily circular', in that it returns African Caribbean people not to Africa but to 'what Africa has *become* in the New World, what we have made of "Africa"'.[19] Journeys in *Meet Me in Mozambique* lack this sense of cultural weight and of becoming. As I have argued, Markham's selection of Mozambique as a setting for his stories is at once teasingly suggestive and, at the same time, markedly non-symbolic when it comes to the tracing of a black British cultural heritage. Additionally, Pewter's journeys are characterized more by hesitation and delay than by progression; a less productive version of Hall's 'necessarily circular' journey can be seen in his fruitless 'detour to the post office' (p. 160), which results in a missed flight. Significantly, Pewter does not 'find himself' in Africa; his search for his elusive alter-ego, Colin Retford, proves futile. Not getting to the point becomes the organizing principle of both Pewter's journeys and the stories which feature him.

As mentioned above, *Meet Me in Mozambique* combines a divergent narrative structure with a 'roundabout approach' to self-writing (p. 30). In his essay, 'Autobiography in the Third Person', Philippe Lejeune looks at the kind of autobiography where a writer presents himself through the eyes of another as a means of 'retriev[ing] or modify[ing] the image he thinks others have of him'.[20] He argues that this strategy, which he terms 'detour', allows 'one's public image [to] be molded while leaving all the private image [sic] in the shadows'.[21] Lejeune's notion of 'detour' offers a basis for reading Markham's self-parody in *Meet Me in Mozambique* as an indirect mode of autobiography, and, as such, a form of digression. Markham explores external constructions of himself in the writing of the stories. For example, the reciprocal 'send[ing] up' (p. 83) of Pewter, Retford, and Carrington offers a satirical take on Markham and his writing process from various angles. The strategy of 'detour' enables Markham to portray himself as if from the outside, and in doing so to manipulate his public image.

This becomes clearer if we look in detail at Markham's characterization of Pewter alongside and against another one of his alter-egos, Michael Carrington. In 'Notes at Maputo Airport', Pewter reflects:

> I was pretty certain that what I was looking for wasn't *root*. I wasn't with the African-Americans and West Indian intellectuals on that quest, which seemed to me to play largely into the hands of the white-skinned ethnics at home who liked to pretend that we didn't belong here. (p. 169)

With this self-conscious statement, Pewter positions himself directly against the role assumed by Carrington in the earlier story, 'Irish Potatoes', set at a conference in Uganda. We are told that, at the conference, Carrington had 'posed as a messenger ... between one group out there, in the diaspora, and people here, at home, so to speak' (p. 48). Carrington's visit to Uganda is therefore framed as a voyage 'home', the purpose of which is to identify his ancestral roots. 'Irish Potatoes' is narrated by Pewter, and features Carrington as a third person protagonist. The textual power relations ensuing from this arrangement are explored thematically through allusions to a relationship characterized both by alliance and antagonism. Carrington discovers that an academic in the literature department owns a selection of his plays, and verifies with her that they are 'The Pewter Stapleton edition' (p. 53). By presenting them as collaborators on a literary text, Markham indicates that both characters are facets of himself. However, on the following page we discover that at the conference Carrington 'had wickedly sought to drop his old friend Pewter Stapleton in it' (p. 54) by criticizing his handling of a politically sensitive topic.

Carrington's mockery of Pewter's way of thinking is reciprocated in Pewter's implicit critique of Carrington's ideas, as he narrates his story. Carrington appears to have a clearer sense of himself as a 'black' writer than Pewter. At the conference, he talks of 'the early days of making theatre in Britain, the 1950s, then in the Caribbean – putting a black image across, what sort of black image you put across, sort of thing'. He also mentions 'adapting the classics … just as Soyinka and Mustapha Matura had done' (p. 54). These comments imply that Carrington is building his profile as a writer on the basis of racial identifications: the 'black image' becomes more important than his Montserrat background. Pewter traces a genealogy of literary influence back to the Caribbean, identifying with St. Caesarean cultural figures based on his teacher in Montserrat and the Tobagonian poet, Eric Roach. In contrast, Carrington aligns himself on racial terms with a Nigerian writer and a black British, Trinidad-born writer. Carrington is also more commercially successful as a writer than Pewter, a fact which inspires in Pewter both envy and derision. In 'On the Death of C.J. Harris', Pewter realizes that 'they had chosen Carrington over him' to write a eulogy 'because Carrington was the safe choice. Fearless, iconoclastic Carrington was held to be safer than bookish Pewter' (p. 76). Paradoxically, Carrington's iconoclasm fits neatly into the socio-cultural climate of postwar Britain, unlike Pewter's densely allusive literary games, and his tendency to '[talk] round the subject' (p. 18) of racism rather than tackling it directly. Adopting a straightforwardly confrontational stance, Carrington produces more marketable material than Pewter, who refuses to 'play along' with what is expected of him as a black British writer (p. 76). In 'send[ing] up' Carrington through Pewter,

Markham is able to explore the role of the politicized black writer while maintaining an ironic distance from it.

Although it is possible to interpret Markham's narrative strategies in terms of Lejeune's concept of 'detour', the stories in *Meet Me in Mozambique* challenge and renegotiate this theoretical model. For Lejeune, in situations where an author '*pretends* to speak about himself as someone else might, by using the third person or by inventing a fictive narrator', this takes place 'within the framework of a text controlled by an autobiographical pact'.[22] He makes the following argument:

> The ostentatious display of multiple postures ... is only possible if identity is still postulated by the reading contract. The more the autobiographer makes the great leap, the more he needs to establish, on some other level, what he is departing from.[23]

According to this model, deviation from first person narration in autobiography is necessarily accompanied by a reinforcement of the authorial voice; even in the act of detour, the writer anticipates an end point where the identities of author, narrator, and protagonist will be reconciled. In Markham's stories, however, the process of detour is extended indefinitely. As we have seen in the 'Irish Potatoes' story, dissension between a first person narrator and a third person protagonist – both textual versions of Markham – is taken to extremes, becoming a central theme of the story as well as a structuring device. In subsequent stories, this gap only widens as Carrington and Retford actively seek to escape Pewter's grasp. By withholding the use of his own name in using semi-autobiographical narrators and protagonists, Markham allows them to develop identities markedly distinct from, although linked to, his own. Through this proliferation of fictional personae, readers lose sight of the author. In the writing of *Meet Me in Mozambique*, then, Markham breaches the terms of Lejeune's 'autobiographical pact'.

In moving beyond the limits of the genre set by Lejeune, Markham's work opens up new possibilities for autobiography. Studies of life-writing in postcolonial contexts have emphasized the significance of fiction-making in the writing of the self. In an essay entitled 'Edward Said and the Fiction of Autobiography', Tobias Döring considers autobiography as a 'threshold genre', crossing boundaries between 'fact and fiction, memory and history, selves and others'.[24] Building on Paul de Man's notion that autobiography can 'produce and determine the life',[25] Döring makes a case for autobiographies as 'primarily performative texts', in that they are 'not just descriptive, but productive'.[26] In the case of Edward Said's memoir *Out of Place* (1999), he argues, fiction becomes the means by which the writer escapes the 'Edward-self with the foolish English name' and the 'self constructed by parents and social circumstance'.[27] A comparable idea of autobiography as a continuous process of self-revision is put forward by Leigh Gilmore, who identifies in Jamaica Kincaid's writing a practice of 'serial autobiography' through which she challenges colonial models of identity.[28] Viewing autobiography as 'an opportunity to experiment with becoming a person', Gilmore claims that serial autobiography 'permits the writer to take multiple runs at self-representation'.[29] As a result, the self produced through the writing is endlessly extendible.[30]

In *Meet Me in Mozambique*, fiction plays a similarly constitutive role in the writing of the self. Both Carrington and Pewter share elements of Markham's character and life history, but neither figure is purely representational. Like Markham, Carrington is from Montserrat, and has been involved in theatre in Britain and the Caribbean.[31] Pewter is from the fictional island of St. Caesare, supposedly Montserrat's neighbour, but his academic post at Sheffield Hallam University aligns him with the later part of Markham's biography. Pewter performs Markham's writing self in a way which exaggerates his shortcomings, as his unending prevaricatory activities of erasing emails and checking the post forestall any significant plot development.[32] By contrast, the successful, high-profile playwright Carrington could be seen as a hypothetical embodiment of what Markham might have become had he taken a different exit off the roundabout, to return to my earlier metaphor. Neither of these two divergent courses is identical to Markham's, since his reputation as both a failed playwright and an acclaimed poet contains elements of both.[33] Taking into account Döring's and Gilmore's conception of autobiographical writing as producing an ever-changing textual self, I propose that the play of narrative voices in *Meet Me in Mozambique* is autobiographical, not as an accurate portrayal of the author's experiences, but rather as an experimentation with roles not necessarily encompassed by those experiences.

In his memoir, Markham observes how labels such as 'black' can 'entrap you in a too-narrow space' in a way which 'den[ies] or de-emphasize[s] your other selves'.[34] The stories in the collection attend to this concern, complementing and complicating Markham's public image as a black British writer with a variety of 'other selves', all of which are intent on 'upstag[ing]' each other (p. 50). In Lejeune's view, 'the elasticity of the "I" has its limits'.[35] Markham's digressive mode of self-writing tests these limits, distending the "I" and thus creating a flexible subject position. By splitting his authorial voice across a series of narrative personae, Markham deflects any attempt to fix him within a particular identity category or political position. In this way, his violation of Lejeune's autobiographical 'reading contract' is accompanied by an infringement of what Mercer defines as the 'contractual model of subjectivity' imposed on black artists who are obliged to reconcile their style and subject matter with their '"accountability" to the community'.[36] However, while Markham's resistance to the prescribed social responsibility of the black artist resonates with Mercer's, it is not identical. Writing in 2005, Markham's struggle with the 'burden of representation' reacts against different kinds of pressures to those outlined by Mercer in his discussion of black cultural production in the 1970s and 1980s. James Procter examines how black writing in these two decades was characterized by 'a realist aesthetics privileging "transparency", "immediacy" and "authenticity"'. He compares this to developments in the period from the late 1980s into the twenty-first century, when 'realism was displaced by increasingly experimental self-consciousness'.[37] Markham's experimental self-writing positions him within this later generation of writers who not only refuse the representative role of 'speaking for' a marginalized community, but also question the assumption that their work reflects an authentic, extra-textual self.

Whereas Mercer considers that black artists might recognize 'the violence entailed in speaking *for* others' by 'speak[ing] *from* the specificity of experience',[38] Markham finds the latter mode of writing similarly constrictive. In *Meet Me in Mozambique*, he neither accepts the role of spokesperson for a community nor restricts his writing to the 'specificity' of his personal experience. Reflecting upon his invention of the adventurous action-hero, Colin Retford, Pewter explains that his reason for creating a fictional self 'conspicuously unlike [him]self' was to 'give up the safe ground' and 'shift the norm towards greater risk – emotional, moral, physical, whatever – than I possessed' (p. 236). Following Bruce King's reading of Markham's multiple 'disguises' as 'a way to avoid racial categorization with its accompanying expectations as to subject matter, diction, and attitude',[39] I suggest that by inhabiting roles removed from his own, Markham deliberately provokes those readers who seek in his work an authentic expression of black British identity. In 'Seminar on the Frank Worrell Roundabout, Barbados', Eye See Eye's highly marketable 'authenticity' as an African Caribbean writer is exposed as no more than a mask worn for the benefit of critics and publishers. Markham's refusal to offer such a performance in *Meet Me in Mozambique* certainly carries a 'risk', in that it could be interpreted as an attempt to shirk social responsibility. However, there is an ethical dimension to this act of non-compliance. Markham's persistent questioning of the label 'black' and the ways in which it has been applied invites readers to scrutinize our own assumptions regarding the style, content, and politics of black British writing.

NOTES

1. E.A. Markham, 'Seminar on the Frank Worrell Roundabout, Barbados', in *Taking the Drawing Room Through Customs: Selected Stories (1972–2002)* (Leeds: Peepal Tree Press, 2002), pp. 172–80 (p. 174).
2. Markham, 'Seminar on the Frank Worrell Roundabout, Barbados', p. 173.
3. E.A. Markham, *Meet Me in Mozambique* (Birmingham: Tindall Street Press, 2005). All further references are to this edition and are included in the text.
4. E.A. Markham, *Against the Grain: A 1950s Memoir* (Leeds: Peepal Tree Press, 2008), pp. 128–29.
5. Markham, *Against the Grain*, p. 145.
6. Alison Donnell, 'Introduction', in *Companion to Contemporary Black British Culture* (London: Routledge, 2002), pp. xii–xvi (p. xii).
7. Donnell, 'Introduction', p. xiii.
8. Donnell, 'Introduction', p. xiv.
9. Kobena Mercer, *Welcome to the Jungle: New Positions in Black Cultural Studies* (London and New York: Routledge, 1994), p. 235.
10. Mercer, *Welcome to the Jungle*, p. 240.
11. Mercer, *Welcome to the Jungle*, p. 250.
12. E.A. Markham, 'Roots and Roots', *PN Review*, January/February 2003 (a lecture delivered at the Literature of the Commonwealth Festival, Manchester, 2002), 22–28 (p. 22).
13. See 'Chapter Four: Inside Government House', in Markham, *Against the Grain*, pp. 58–72.
14. Markham, 'Seminar on the Frank Worrell Roundabout, Barbados', p. 175.
15. John McLeod, 'Fantasy Relationships: Black British Canons in a Transnational World', in *A Black British Canon?* eds, Gail Low and Marion Wynne Davies (Basingstoke, HT: Palgrave Macmillan, 2006), pp. 93–104 (p. 100).
16. McLeod, 'Fantasy Relationships', p. 98.
17. For example, in 'Meet Me in Mozambique' Pewter's train from London to Sheffield is diverted via Doncaster (p. 241), and in 'On the Game' Retford is held up in South Africa 'en route' from Mozambique to England (p. 144).
18. Paul Gilroy, *The Black Atlantic: Modernity and Double Consciousness* (London and New York: Verso, 1993), p. 17.
19. Stuart Hall, 'Cultural Identity and Diaspora', in *Identity: Community, Culture, Difference*, ed., Jonathan Rutherford (London: Lawrence & Wishart, 1990), pp. 222–37 (pp. 231–32).
20. Philippe Lejeune, 'Autobiography in the Third Person', *New Literary History*, 9:1 (1977) 27–50, p. 41.
21. Lejeune, 'Autobiography in the Third Person', p. 43.
22. Lejeune, 'Autobiography in the Third Person', p. 27.

23. Lejeune, 'Autobiography in the Third Person', p. 40.
24. Tobias Döring, 'Edward Said and the Fiction of Autobiography', *Wasafiri*, 21:2 (2006) 71–78, p. 72.
25. Paul de Man, 'Autobiography as De-facement', *Modern Language Notes*, 94:5 (1979) 919–30, p. 920.
26. Döring, 'Edward Said and the Fiction of Autobiography', p. 71.
27. Döring, 'Edward Said and the Fiction of Autobiography', p. 74.
28. Leigh Gilmore, 'Endless Autobiography? Jamaica Kincaid and Serial Autobiography', in *Postcolonialism and Autobiography*, eds, Alfred Hornung and Ernstpeter Ruhe (Amsterdam and Atlanta, GA: Rodopi, 1998), pp. 211–31 (p. 211).
29. Gilmore, 'Endless Autobiography?', p. 217.
30. Gilmore, 'Endless Autobiography?', p. 215.
31. In 1970–1971 Markham spent a year as director of the Caribbean Theatre Workshop, travelling to St Vincent, Montserrat, and Trinidad. See Greg C. Winston, 'EA. Markham', in *British and Irish Short Fiction Writers, 1945-2000*, eds, Cheryl Alexander Malcolm and David Malcolm (Detroit, MI: Thompson Gale, 2006), pp. 197–205 (p. 199).
32. This aspect of Pewter's character is displayed most pointedly in 'The Dakota Club', partially set in Sheffield, where Pewter recovers from a cataract operation and corresponds from a distance with the much more active and constructively engaged Colin Retford.
33. In *Against the Grain*, Markham himself offers a self-deprecatory account of his aspirations as a playwright in the 1950s and 1960s before he made the decision to focus on poetry, acknowledging the weaknesses of plays with 'no action, no movement towards crisis, and no sense that the people involved are engaged in any dilemma that matters'. He observes that 'it is easy now to understand the endless rejection letters that greeted my plays over the years' (p. 127).
34. Markham, *Against the Grain*, p. 147.
35. Lejeune, 'Autobiography in the Third Person', pp. 39–40.
36. Mercer, *Welcome to the Jungle,* p. 240.
37. James Procter, *Dwelling Places: Postwar Black British Writing* (Manchester and New York: Manchester UP, 2003), p. 11.
38. Mercer, *Welcome to the Jungle*, p. 250.
39. Bruce King, *The Internationalization of English Literature* (Oxford: Oxford UP, 2004), pp. 115–16.

Across the Indian Ocean: Chinese Hybridity in South Africa

TANYA CHAN-SAM

In the snatches of autobiographical commentary that follow, I illustrate the degree of Chinese hybridity in South Africa. My family history has long been connected to that nation. Our stories date from the nineteenth century and we had a peculiarly complex relationship to the apartheid categories of 'African' and 'Coloured'. These stories describe Chinese social experience in Black South African society at a time when the apartheid regime aimed to keep the various communities separate. By way of this autobiographical commentary, I wish to explore to some extent the complexities of South African society, a society that has an element of Chinese hybridity at its heart.[1]

There has been contact between China and Africa across the Indian Ocean as far back as the early fifteenth century, but systematic migration only began in the mid-nineteenth century. Much of this movement was related to the demand for colonial labour, the so-called 'coolie trade', especially after the abolition of slavery. The 'coolie trade' was highly regulated and most workers were sent back to their countries of origin after their contracts expired. Following the discovery of gold in 1888, many Cantonese and Hakka Chinese travelled to South Africa. Land shortages back in China also encouraged them to look for a new life elsewhere. These migrants were generally male and the demand for labour came primarily from the mining sector. Other small but enterprising groups of independent traders serviced Chinese labour migrants and undertook small-scale exports.

My great-grandfather arrived in South Africa in 1891, after journeying across the Indian Ocean from Guangdong. Like many of his fellow travellers, he had heard of the discovery of gold in South Africa and was in search of his fortune. He used to tell the following story about his first disembarkation at Durban docks.

'Naam?' barked the customs official.

'Hau Chan Sau.'

The customs official replaced his pen in the inkwell. He hung his big blond head, showing only his scalp to the man standing in front of his desk. The head swayed to and fro like a bull ready to charge. The queue of men fanned out behind Hau Chan Sau to observe the goings on, their faces creased with worry. My great-grandfather removed his travel documents from his jacket pocket.

The official's chair creaked as he leaned back, glanced up. He took the papers, tutting in irritation. They quivered slightly. The official took up his pen and dipped it three, four times in the inkwell; the taps audible against the thick glass. The official wrote with his fingers clumped into a fist. The nib of his pen hovered over the roman letters above the Chinese characters. The tip of his tongue protruded. Then he said, 'Now look here, I'll jus' change the u to two r's, add a y.' He looked up. 'You nogal look like a Harry.'

The official bent down and addressed the paper again. 'And what do you need a middle name for? I never use mine.' One stroke of blue scored out the Chan.

'And this surname of yours, ag no man, I can't even say it. Jus change the u to m. And there, Harry Sam, that's better.'

Hau Chan Sau had expected many changes, had stayed awake long into the night on the boat trip from China dreaming of his new life in South Africa. But he hadn't anticipated this. All gone. His father's name, his own name, his clan name. Three thousand years of naming systems wiped out in a stroke. Harry stared at the line of blue through Chan, his clan name.

'Put back Chan.'

He spoke quietly. In the queue behind Harry, eyes narrowed, fists balled, knuckles whitened. The customs official scanned the faces of the men that were squeezed into the tiny customs office. He levered himself up to look in the direction of the supervisor's office. His supervisor glared back from behind the glass and held his fob watch high. The customs official bent his head and, in cramped letters, wrote *Chan* in front of the crossed out version.

Harry smiled as he took back the papers.

A family name is priceless in any society. It attaches the individual to a lineage. It indicates the region or country of origin. It marks identity and signifies status. Decades later, I asked my great-grandfather why he had not fought to keep his own name, or his father's name.

'Those names are not important', he said. 'I have many names in my life: *boy*, *sonny*, anything. My father too. A man can have many fathers with many names, but you only have one clan name. That is the important one. That is the one you fight to keep. Always.'

South African Coloured communities are hybrid by their very nature. So, too, are Chinese names and physical features found all over South Africa. A contributory factor to this racial mix could be the itinerant hawkers who travelled to outlying districts selling their wares in the early twentieth century. These hawkers were known as 'paper sons'. This name refers to the practice of Chinese traders, who would sponsor young men to travel from China to destinations such as South Africa, the United States, and Britain by claiming, on official documents, that they were their sons. In reality, paper sons were often clansmen who were indentured to their sponsor until they paid off the cost of their travel, accommodation, and other expenses associated with setting them up in a new country.

'D' was a paper son of Harry Chan-Sam. He was a clansman from the same village and was invited to South Africa by his 'father', who belonged to a consortium of Chinese businessmen who acted as guarantors, sponsors, and employees of paper sons. In return for acting in this capacity, Harry received a loan to set up a business, usually a shop. D worked to repay Harry by touring the outlying parts of the Eastern Cape, staying in small townships or homesteads for one or two nights, selling vegetables, cloth, pots and pans. He claimed to have fathered children in every smallholding and, when D died, several dozen children and grandchildren attended his funeral, all bearing their father's features.

When the People's Republic of China was formed in 1949, emigration was officially brought to an end and restrictions were placed on people joining their existing families overseas. After 1948, the apartheid regime in South Africa classified the Chinese as non-white (Coloured). With few other options available to them, many Chinese remained in South Africa. Many were already living and working in black townships.

In apartheid South Africa, any person with a Chinese surname was racially classified as Coloured or even 'Chinese-coloured'. The pre-apartheid Chinese community, which was overwhelmingly male, was already restricted to trading in black townships in British-ruled, colonial South Africa. These men took local wives, had children, and continued to work and live in black townships throughout the apartheid years. They held widely different views and attitudes from their offspring regarding identity. Some chose to associate closely with other Chinese communities. Others adopted African and Coloured society as their own. However, for some, there was yet another option. Since the Japanese were classified as 'honorary whites', there was much confusion in the classification of the Chinese. This confusion allowed many Chinese to enter white society. 'Uncle Y', who was the son of my great-grandfather's cousin, opted to become 'white' in apartheid South Africa. He took his mother's surname. She was classified as Coloured, but her surname was more acceptably anglicized, and she had fair skin, which Uncle Y had inherited. He married a white woman and, when their children were born, they had Chinese features. Afraid of being classified Coloured in the apartheid era, he rationalized the children's physical features as being inherited from a distant Slavic relative on his wife's side.

In a Western context, Chinese identity is often perceived as homogenous unless there are children from, say, white/Chinese parents. Hybridity results from the mixing of putatively distinct phenomena. In South Africa, hybridity is largely due to the classification of the Chinese as Coloured during the apartheid era. But mixed Chinese identity is not restricted to the Coloured community alone. African Chinese unions are evident among many African communities. This is apparent in the facial features of many individual South Africans. It frequently happens that dominant physical characteristics do not correspond to Chinese surnames so that a person with a Chinese surname may look Coloured, African, or Caucasian. The father of 'Cousin K', for example, was Chinese and his mother was Xhosa. Cousin K has Chinese features with African hair and colouring. His identity is Xhosa yet he has a Chinese surname. In present day South Africa, K has opted to change his Chinese surname to his mother's Xhosa name. He says this ensures his children never have to live as he did, 'on the margin of the margins'.

'T' holds a different view. He is enthusiastic about his multiple identity. T is third generation Chinese African. He continues to run a grocer shop in the African township where his grandfather, a younger cousin of Harry Chan-Sam, first settled. T retains his Chinese family name and has incorporated African names into his children's names. His eldest son is called Tim Chan Rohihlahla, and was named after Tim's hero, Nelson Rohihlahla Mandela.

Today I watch 'C' serve her customers at the Chinese Butchery in Joburg. She speaks to them in a mixture of Cantonese, English, and Afrikaans:

'Wai dim aa, wat koop jy vandag? What you buy today?'

'I koop ten rand zyu yuk sausages, pork sausage,' comes the reply.

As she wraps the sausages in white butchers' paper, C explains that her customers are a mix of local Coloured people and newly-arrived Chinese immigrants. C learned Cantonese from her Chinese grandmother, who was brought to South Africa from Guangdong in 1950 as a young bride just before China closed its borders and imposed travel restrictions. C's grandmother was married to C's mixed heritage grandfather. C is proud of her Coloured identity and says she does not experience any sense of crisis. Her children are Coloured, as is her husband. Her family's butcher business was started by her great-grandfather, a Chan clansman, who arrived on the same boat as Harry Chan-Sam. The two men became 'cousins' and supported one another's efforts. She delights in practising her Chinese language skills as much as she loves teaching colloquial Afrikaans to new Chinese immigrant traders who are eager to learn the language as they assimilate into Coloured society, building their own businesses and living in post-apartheid South Africa.

The Chinese gained full South African citizenship in 1994. Yet they were excluded from business concessions made to benefit previously disadvantaged groups under affirmative action, which was termed Black Economic Empowerment legislation. In a landmark ruling on 18 June 2008, the Pretoria High Court afforded the Chinese the same racial status as Black and Indian South Africans. Chinese South Africans are now recognized as previously disadvantaged citizens of South Africa.

Like my forebears, I too migrated, leaving South Africa to live in Yorkshire. Here, my accent is the first characteristic that singles me out as South African. Surprise is often expressed at my surname and perplexed glances confirm that I am not perceived as Chinese. Explaining my mixed race heritage sometimes eases the confusion. I search for signs of hybridity in others, particularly in those with a Chinese background. When I encounter other Chinese identities, I remember the textured nature of my own, for which no ethnic monitoring form is adequate. That is why the task of describing Chinese hybridity is best left to biographers and storytellers.

NOTES

1. For general reference on this topic see Darryl Accone, *All Under Heaven: The Story of a Chinese Family in South Africa* (Johannesburg, David Philip, 2003); and Lynn Pan, *Sons of the Yellow Emperor: The Story of the Overseas Chinese* (New York. Kodansha America, 1994).

   see: <http://www.news24.com/City_Press/Finance/0,186-246_2351551,00.html>

IAN DUHIG

After Ovid

I.M. DAVID OLUWALE

Ovid prayed that those gods love become gods
and hung fresh wreaths on branches of the trees
which Baucis and Philemon were changed into
at the same moment the old couple died.
To save both from the pain of either's loss,
they'd begged this gift from gods who, when disguised,
the kindly pair took in, warmed up and fed –
their door the last these gods tried in their town,
finding every other closed against them.
But masked gods walk among us as a test
for hospitality's our sacred duty;
nor will locked doors keep out that punishment
gods visit on those shunning unknown visitors,
who'd turn cold eyes on all in need or lost.
On the high ground, Baucis and Philemon's
small home was safe when their whole town was lost –
more: it then grew marble floors, colonnades,
an altar, pediment and golden roof
while neighbours' tears, withheld for homeless gods,
now swelled the tidal wave that rose and fell
on mansion, hovel, counting-house and church,
a flood as levelling as that great flood
when dead fish seemed to perch like birds in trees
or wreaths laid by respectful votaries
while underneath waves billowed like blown wheat
on wheatfields yielding only anchor-holds,
as if the Aire became that element
it sounded always destined to become,
a change to take the breath away from men.

River Mask

The first and most constant problem with the City of Leeds is to find it. There never was a more faceless city or a more deceptive one. It hasn't a face because it has too many, all of them different.
Patrick Nuttgens, *Leeds: The Back to Front, Inside-Out, Upside-Down City*

A spirit of the air and river Aire,
I took a constitutional in Leeds
to reconnoitre for a future flood
then find out why a wise man called the place
the Back to Front, Inside-Out, Upside-Down
City when through my water looking-glass
it's just as I'd imagine dry land life.
As time means nothing to me, in no time
I got to know it back-to-front etc.
to like and dislike its stark contradictions,
its masks and antimasks, blunt truths and lies,
its meanness and its generosity:
I felt at home, being changeable myself –
as Oshun, I might want my water fresh:
as Jenny Greenteeth, I prefer it foul;
'reflection' means a thing and its reverse.
To most round here I'm the River of Life
but to some my waters are Babylon's,
and Leeds is hated for its foreigners,
the 'Holy City' nickname's for its Jews
to such as call it now 'Jihad HQ'
and darker guests got worse than hurtful names ...
Now honoured thus
With all his beauteous race,
Who though but black in face
Yet are they bright
And full of life and light,
To prove that beauty best
Which not the colour, but the feature
Assures unto the creature.
That's 'The Masque of Blackness' by Ben Jonson
inventor of the outcasts' antimasque
we're taking off for David Oluwale,
the saddest city sacrifice to me,
whose surname's Yoruba for 'God Comes Home' –

to God's Own County: what could be more right? –
whose last home was this Holy City's centre,
the final circle of his Christian hell,
a web of streets that brought him to my arms
though he was always terrified of water,
driven to this by two men of the law.
Travelling through this parallel universe,
for a circle-dance in David's memory
for memories blank as faces, in blank verse,
a mask of whiteness as in 'wash' or 'rose',
I choose that chariot of paradox,
the zero-fare City Centre Loop Bus.
Free bus rides in Yorkshire! the bigot gasps;
the cynic learns that nothing is a price
beyond all reckoning in pounds and pence.
It's called the 'Asylum Seekers' Express'
by those who like to keep their England little.
The Loop Bus tours our Holy City centre,
stopping for the Crypt, a homelessness shelter
David didn't stop at, being black:
no Fanon mask of whiteness, think Nietzsche,
how gratitude is hatred in a mask,
so David didn't feign it at the last.
Beyond some outposts of the NHS,
which locked up David for a decade then
evicted him to live rough on these streets,
the bus turns by a bar which is a boat
then Clay Pit Lane of Hepworth's, where Ken Kitching,
gaoled for David's torture, worked in security ...
An old school cop, he ruled the streets of Leeds
to St Paul's killing letter of the law,
black and white as Harrison's parish church,
skirted by our bus which turns beyond it
and this theatre, to Millgarth Police Station,
where David took more beatings in his turn,
whose own beat swung as this too near my home
where I reflect on David's journey still
in a city not given to reflection.
Be silent now, the ceremony's done ...

Note 'River Mask' is spoken by the Interlocutor of 'God Comes Home', a dramatic piece co-written with Rommi Smith and performed immediately before Dipo Agboluaje's play at West Yorkshire Playhouse, directly opposite Millgarth Police Station where David Oluwale was regularly beaten. The Interlocutor links testimony recorded from asylum seekers and immigrants in Leeds with other creative passages and monologues.

The Holy City

I recently gave what felt like one of the least-enjoyed poetry readings since one of Nero's, though in post-imperial Morley rather than imperial Rome. Morley is a proud small town with its own Mayor on the edge of Leeds, the city where I have lived on and off for nearly thirty years. Things had started well: this very Mayor had turned out to welcome me and Kester Aspden. Kester was reading from his acclaimed *Nationality: Wog: The Hounding of David Oluwale*, a meticulously-researched account, using newly-released government documents, of a Nigerian college graduate dying homeless on the streets of Leeds in 1969, after prolonged abuse at the hands of two its policemen. Our reading was a benefit for the Oluwale Memorial Appeal, but raised a derisory amount – small wonder, perhaps, given that Morley has the greatest concentration of BNP membership in the UK, as I discovered on examining their leaked membership list. In itself, this list evinces a limited success for that quasi-romantic 'Merrie-England' nationalism which the BNP tries to project sometimes, with one member describing himself as a witch (presumably a recruiting agent is responsible for the comment that he 'could be an embarrassment if active'); another calls herself a 'pre-Raphaelite style portrait painter', while a third is keen to advertise the fact that he possessed two suits of mediaeval armour, and is available for 'jousting at rallies'.

At Leeds Bus Station on the way back, you get to contemplate Millgarth Police Station, another station of the God-fearing Oluwale's cross. After his body turned up in the Aire under mysterious circumstances (Oluwale was frightened of water), his tormentors were turned in by police cadet Gary 'Gazzer' Galvin, an eighteen-year-old living with his parents in Tony Harrison's Beeston, who were immigrants from County Clare. On the headstone of Oluwale's pauper's grave in Killingbeck Cemetery there are ten surnames, the first four of which are Flanagan, McHale, Lynch and Mahoney. Leeds is disliked for many reasons, and one of them is because it has had significant immigration over several centuries; its old nicknames of 'the Holy City' and 'the Jerusalem of the North' are anti-Semitic sneers – more recently its terms of abuse are along the lines of 'Jihad Northern HQ'. The bus that takes me home up Chapeltown Road passes through an area which is a palimpsest of immigration; as each community in turn gets settled and successful, it moves up this road in the general direction of Harrogate. I want to give some brief consideration to one aspect of the cultural life of its shrinking Irish community, as a way of throwing light on the idea of a 'devolved' and regionally-inflected migrant experience in a small way, but this is the only way such a regional picture can be built up.

I'd like to start this by quoting from Donald MacRaild's *Culture, Conflict and Migration*: 'historians, like the Irish themselves, need to fan out from the classical centres ... to consider new areas of importance'. He was talking about less urban places than Leeds, but the migrant I want to advance as artistically important came to Leeds from Mayo via London, fanning out as MacRaild describes. His name was Dudley Kane, but is better known under the stage name of Darach Ó Catháin, given to him by Seán Ó Riada, who considered him the finest sean-nós singer of his generation (you can listen to him as Darach on Youtube). Sean-nós ('old style') is a highly elaborate type of traditional Irish unaccompanied singing, distinguished by melismatic and intervallic ornamentation and such stylistic features as the glottal stop which is alien to many neighbouring singing disciplines but often found in those of the Indian subcontinent, in common with many other aspects of traditional Irish culture, something Seán Ó Riada lectured on many times.

In truth, I don't need to make any claims on his behalf as his status is so firmly established, as witnessed by the recent RTÉ programme about him and his family in Leeds. I'd listen to him in a few Irish pubs in lower Chapeltown, where I was told I could hear more All-Ireland Champions on their respective instruments than in any pub over there. Local eccentricities could flourish, such as the Presbyterian uilleann piper nicknamed 'Twoice' (because he was always telling people he was 'twoice' All-Ireland piping champion). His political views followed those of his religion rather than his art and he was a staunch Unionist, and not frightened to advise people of this during heated arguments. However, these were interchanges that were simply too dangerous to have risked on home ground. Protestant Irish emigrants tend to suffer from 'ethnic fade', especially in societies like the USA, where within a few generations they are culturally indistinguishable from the host community. I couldn't comment on this locally, but while the Irish community in the USA has a tendency to turn in itself, parodying what it takes to be 'real Irish', in the first generation of children to these Leeds musicians as they grew up – and if they played – something interesting happened. This is demonstrated by the comment made during a Karen Tweed and Ian Carr 'Folkworld' interview: 'People in Ireland talk about a Leeds style, that they play in Leeds and that you can tell is from Leeds, but it's Irish music.' More particularly, the cognoscenti talk of Paul Ruane's 'Leeds/Sligo style', as the cultural influence of the new community ramifies.

Of course, the Irish influence on the new environment is significant too; in *The Irish Contribution to English Traditional Tunes*, Francesca Allinson writes of how the latter became 'saturated' with the former. The technicalities are described by Samuel Bayard:

> The English style is characterised by a certain solidity of melodic build and emphasis throughout the tune on the strong notes of the mode, like the tonic or dominant tones, and by preference for the sort of melodic movement which 'gets somewhere' ... the English singer's leaning to relatively straightforward and simple melodic lines is counteracted in Irish tradition by love of ornament, of multiplying notes, of varying rhythmic patterns by this sort of multiplication.

Bayard believes these ornamental tendencies give Irish music a 'wavering and unemphatic movement', lingering on certain notes or tones and repeating them, 'thus impeding the course of the melody'. I would like to take his observations on Irish music and shift them into literature, where I believe a 'wavering and unemphatic movement' of narrative, with multiplying intervallic digression, is a stylistic feature evident in the work of a number of Irish writers, from Laurence Sterne through Oscar Wilde and Flann O'Brien on to Paul Muldoon.

In 2003, as International Writer Fellow at Trinity College Dublin, I was asked to organize an event investigating the literary links between the Republic of Ireland and the North of England. Predictably they were strong: Professor Stephen Matterson's contribution described how, as he grew up in the North-east of England in the 1960s, people interested in poetry there felt closer to developments in Ireland than the Oxbridge/ London dominated South. These links and influences go back a long way and are not always appreciated in their effects; in an interview with Peter Bell, Basil Bunting referred to Geordie as 'a bastard language ... a mixture mainly of south Northumbrian with the Irish that was brought in by the labourers'. The class dimension is important to emphasize; we would not expect professional jargon to show the Roma and Yiddish influences that Northern slang demonstrates, as well as that of the Irish which Bunting so deplored. I have advanced elsewhere the view that Irish music particularly appealed to the Enclosure dispossessed (John Clare collected and played it) for its elegiac qualities, but at the risk of stating the obvious, an art of unaccompanied singing or composition is free.

At the moment in Leeds, a number of writers are collaborating on projects to take place during the run of Oladipo Agboluaje's *The Hounding of David Oluwale*, based on Kester Aspden's book; national organizations like the Poetry Society of Great Britain aren't really active in places like Leeds and it is events like this that gets local poets together. It will involve the testimonies of asylum seekers in the city as well as immigrants, although there is no real distinction between the two in many cases — the Jews who fled here in the past from the Cossacks or Nazis contributed massively to this City, but many of those fleeing Ethiopia or Uganda don't look like they will be given this opportunity. Further, consider the economic circumstances of poetry in different societies, where by an interesting coincidence its existence as a popular art is virtually a sign of poverty (Les Murray has written of how rich countries can't afford poetry). In such regional circumstances, poets like myself will find themselves fortunate enough to be working alongside writers consciously exploring different traditions, like Rommi Smith.

The high regard with which poetry is held in a number of immigrant communities in Leeds has been a shot in the arm for local practitioners, and it is no surprise that Peepal Tree Press should be based in Leeds. It is also notable that there is virtually no influence from other parts of the Anglosphere on the ground here at present either, also for obvious economic reasons. However, in its industrial irrelevance, the weight of individual lives here can have unique impact, as indicated by the cases of David Oluwale and Darach Ó Catháin (the latter now being researched in turn by Kester Aspden for possibly a follow-up book to the one on Oluwale). It would be hard to demonstrate this at a macro-level but we are not engaged in a macro-level exercise. All I can conclude with is to say that somehow this alertness feeds into my reading of, say, Bashō's *Narrow Road to the Deep North*, where he records (in Nobiyuki Yuasa's translation) being invited to stay with Seifū in Obanazawa, 'a rich merchant and yet a man of a truly poetic turn of mind', who lavishes hospitality on him. In an interesting piece of editing, this is immediately followed by a poem by Sora, Bashō's travelling companion, the first verse of which says,

I felt quite at home,
As if it were mine,
Sleeping lazily
In this house of fresh air.

Was Sora not included in Seifū's invitation and having to sleep outside? Whatever the truth of this story, I find myself reading it as a universal sardonic song of those on the road, knights of the road, though not the kind that are available for jousting at rallies.

Michael Gutteridge

COVER ARTIST

Michael Gutteridge has been a great friend of the Moving Manchester project. Described by *Inside and Out* Magazine as an artist who 'lives and breathes Manchester', his paintings are both post-expressionist and surreal. As he explains on his website, despite his love of the countryside, he has a predilection for painting Manchester's cityscapes. He is particularly attracted by what he describes as 'the architecturally diverse mixture of gargoyle-souled Victoriana, modern steel and glass, refurbished Georgian warehouse, 1960s sub-Bauhaus office blocks, and […Manchester's] predominantly lobster-red […] buildings'.[1] He cites Lawrence Stephen Lowry, Chaim Soutine, Edvard Munch, Henri Matisse and Carel Weight as key artistic influences, although he also draws from music and psychology.

In 2006, he created a painting specifically with the Moving Manchester project in mind. Painted in orange-yellow and dark magenta and set against the Midland Hotel and Manchester Central Library in St. Peter's Square, Gutteridge aimed to represent multiracial Manchester. The painting that is featured on the cover of this issue of *Moving Worlds*, 'Tram Between St. Peter's Square and G-Mex', is one of a series of dynamic images depicting Manchester's trams.

Gutteridge describes his paintings as a deliberate 'agitated distortion' of Manchester's buildings. First he photographs the scene that he wishes to paint and then gradually reduces its 'physical actuality', concentrating instead on the buildings' 'sensual vibrancy'. He enjoys painting expressionist-style images but has, with time, become increasingly attracted by 'swirling paint around in a kind of adventurous delight', resisting the instinct to reproduce faithfully what he sees in the attempt to convey the city's 'nervous energy'. The result is a 'Dr Seuss-cat-in-the-hat derangement' that is the outcome of several months' studious concentration.[2]

NOTES

1. <http://www.michaelgutteridge.com/html/info.html> accessed 26 June 2009.
2. <http://www.michaelgutteridge.com/html/manifesto.html> accessed 26 June 2009

HONEY OBEROI VAHALI
Lives in Exile: Exploring the Inner World of Tibetan Refugees
New Delhi: Routledge 2009
ISBN 978 0 415 44606 8 hb 400pp 850 rupees

In the very first sentence of her book, Honey Oberoi Vahali describes what the Chinese communists have done in Tibet since the 1950s as 'a festered wound on the body of the world's conscience'. Much of what generations of Tibetan refugees to India experienced before leaving their homeland is tragically familiar: the systematic abuse of anything to do with their own culture; struggle sessions, beatings, imprisonment and brutal torture; the hardship and deprivations of the escape across the Himalayas.

This book does not deal with politics first and foremost, or even the attempted destruction of a culture, though when speaking of refugees it is of course impossible not to confront the cultural and political circumstances that created them. Vahali herself says, 'As a person who strongly believed in the egalitarian values of socialism, the communist Chinese takeover of Tibet posed a major challenge for me.' But, as a Professor of Psychology and a practising psychotherapist, she is, as the book's subtitle suggests, primarily interested in the inner life of Tibetan refugees. She talks to a wide range of interviewees: an older generation who had grown up in the 'old' Tibet and left around the same time as the Dalai Lama in 1959; the children of that generation, now middle-aged, born in Tibet but brought up in exile in India; the generations born in exile; more recent arrivals, some of them victims of the most appalling torture; refugees who have tried to return 'home' to Tibet only to come back again to India, strangers in their own land; monks and nuns, nomads and political activists. The book allows them to speak in their own voices, tell their own stories, many of them truly harrowing. Then Vahali draws more general conclusions and sometimes makes comparisons with other refugee groups. She has personal as well as professional experience of what she calls the 'ruptured life-histories' of refugees: her own parents and grandparents 'resettled' in India at the time of Partition in 1947. Nor does she shy away from asking awkward questions: 'Is it just a coincidence that 9 of these 10 activists … were persons either from the upper classes or from monastic sects?' – people with more to lose under the new order, in other words.

But what quickly becomes clear is that what differentiates Tibetans from other refugee groups is their Buddhist faith and the love and reverence they feel towards their political and religious leader, the Dalai Lama. One refugee talks about how a single hair of the Dalai Lama, blessed and placed in a locket, gave him strength to survive years of starvation and imprisonment; another of how a small act of kindness could give hope in the nightmare of an environment where 'the pressure to criticize and confess was relentless … you were expected to do harm to your fellow prisoners as if they were your worst enemies'. Some of the testimonies are heart-breakingly moving: 'In opposition to the violence I was being subjected to, I thought of non-violent means of struggle.' Or 'The most painful thing in being tortured was the realization that the torturer was another human being.'

The Dalai Lama's teachings on these topics are extraordinary. We must learn from our oppressors and try to develop compassion towards the Chinese, he says. The Buddhist doctrine of karma teaches that each of us is ultimately responsible for his or her own condition, so the torturers are suffering or will suffer as much as the victims of torture. Vahali summarizes towards the end of the book: 'the real challenge of victimization is not merely in enduring the torture, but of not losing one's humanity in the process of enduring it … Forgiveness does not imply forgetting. It is only in remembering that an inner process, a struggle, to overcome hatred can be initiated.'

The need to remember and to communicate those memories is a theme that runs throughout this book. For many of those interviewed, it is the only thing that can give meaning to all they have endured. Honey Oberoi Vahali's book remembers and interprets and, in so doing, tries to help us to understand the incomprehensible.

David Lascelles, Harewood House Trust

MARTA DVOŘÁK
The Faces of Carnival in Anita Desai's In Custody
Paris: Presses Universitaires de France 2008
ISBN 978 2 13 057108 7 pb 173pp 14 euros

With the exception of student handbooks, few book-length studies of individual postcolonial texts are being published at the moment. Marta Dvořák's thought-provoking study of Anita Desai's *In Custody* bucks this trend. However, the apparently narrow scope of Dvořák's analysis should not be mistaken for a lack of ambition. In this short monograph, close reading becomes the platform for a theoretically sophisticated interpretive approach to transculturality.

One of Dvořák's aims is to 'equip' readers with contextual details that will enrich interpretation of Desai's novel. To this end, her study is packed with information about caste, food, rituals, language, dance and drama in the Indian subcontinent. Such emphasis upon cultural specificity is nothing new. What sets this study apart is Dvořák's argument that *In Custody* is 'exemplary of syncretic transcultural writing'. With this contention comes a sharp challenge to a 'view of alterity as a feature of a material location, rooted in a specific spatial, socio-political, linguistic or religious context'.

In short, Dvořák insists that analysis of transcultural texts must move beyond a bounded notion of cultural context, remaining alert to 'culture-specific' and 'cross-cultural' referents. The logic for such an approach stems from an awareness of Desai's mixed literary heritage, her immersion in European and Indian cultural traditions. However, the implications of this argument reach beyond Desai's writing. Taking Desai as a case in point, Dvořák identifies processes of contact, migration and exchange as a catalyst for cultural development. Indeed, she demonstrates that Desai 'redeploy[s] the vantages and techniques of literary predecessors throughout the globe belonging to aesthetic and philosophical movements which have always migrated, mixed, and mutated'.

Taking cultural translation as her point of departure, Dvořák attends to intertextual patterning in *In Custody*, focusing on three main topics: displacement, creolization, and targeted audience; purity and pollution; and realism, romance, and satire. Perhaps the most rewarding aspect of this short book is its attention to detail. Dvořák's sensitive textual readings shed light on Desai's sustained commitment to a syncretic transnational culture, a tightly woven 'tapestry' comparable to the refined synthesis of Hindu, Muslim, European and Persian themes and techniques in Mughal miniatures. Take, for instance, Dvořák's fascinating discussion of Desai's allusions to Romantic poetry, especially Keats's 'La Belle Dame Sans Merci'. This, of course, is the poem that the great Urdu poet Nur claims as his favourite; he even recites it on a tape recording that is supposed to preserve his life's work for posterity. Attending to Desai's 'recontextualized articulation of a foregrounded, precedingly overlooked cultural overlap', Dvořák identifies a quality of parody in her repetition of canonical texts, not least because Desai unsettles any notion of a fixed, authentic cultural tradition. Undercutting Romantic attachment to original expression, Desai's 'transfiguration' of Keats underlines that the poem is, in fact, a mishmash of familiar narrative elements, or, as Dvořák puts it, 'the figurations which shape colonial cultural paradigms are already refigurations'.

While Dvořák's approach yields fascinating insights about the crisscrossing of cultural influences across the globe, the broad historical and cultural scope of this project, which ranges from Greek tragedy to Zadie Smith, does not come without risks. For one thing, Dvořák appears to embrace a universalism that sometimes threatens to elide the cultural specificity that is so fundamental to her approach. At one point, she calls for a turn away from a critical approach that puts a premium upon cultural difference in favour of a method that derives its coordinates from European philosophers such as Plato and Descartes. In this context, readers might wish for sustained discussion of the political, historical, and economic realities that underpin Desai's hybridity. More generally, striking points are raised without being developed fully. In particular, little is made of Dvořák's astute observation that Desai's indictment, in 'A Secret Connivance', of the 'burden of custom and tradition' which tends to legitimate women's subservience is sharply at odds with her own formal choices, which are, to some degree, dependent upon a reader's knowledge of canonical texts. Notwithstanding these quibbles, this is a lively contribution to recent debates about transculturality, which promises to invigorate discussion of a writer who has received less critical attention in recent years.

Rachel Farebrother, University of Swansea

The Global Village
Edited by Courttia Newland and Monique Roffey
Leeds: Peepal Tree Press 2009
ISBN: 978 1 84523 079 1 pb 212pp £8.99

In his review from 1842 of Nathaniel Hawthorne's *Twice-Told Tales*, Edgar Allan Poe commented on the nature of the 'tale', or short story, which he regarded 'as affording us the best prose opportunity for display of the highest talent'. While the short story form apparently continues to flourish in the United States, this recent volume of short stories, *The Global Village*, begins with the lament that the form has been neglected in the UK for some time. Sadly, it may be difficult to dispute this view. However, Monique Roffey continues with a rather strange claim: 'In 2008, writers would find it easier to sell balls of their hair or small piles of their fingernail clippings than a collection of short stories to a mainstream publisher.' If this is true, the resultant frustration of short story writers might go some way to explaining why so many of the pieces in her jointly edited book are concerned with death – especially of the gruesome, murderous kind. There are some excellent stories in this generous collection; but you may not get to them because, out of the first five stories, those by Olive Senior, Justin Hill and Kay Sexton, are – collectively

– so harrowing, and, frankly, so oddly bloodthirsty, that you may give up and go in pursuit of something altogether less likely to give you nightmares. Bedtime reading this is not.

This is the fourth volume from the Tell Tales Collective, which was established by Courttia Newland in 2004 in response to the dwindling popularity of the short story form in Britain. The theme – 'the global village' – prompted 150 entries, which were whittled down to 26. We are promised that the collection is both 'dark' and 'funny', but there is surprisingly little humour in these stories; instead of laughs, we are given bodies. As Roffey calculates: 'I counted seven deaths (mostly grisly murders), four drug-related stories, two ghost-related stories, one tale of the aftermath of genocide, one tale of the aftermath of the war in Yugoslavia.' Although there is an admission that the editors' tastes were for the 'grim', she claims that 'Together, these stories form the composite picture-of-our-times we were looking for: a zeitgeist collection which reflects the ideas and concerns of writers all over the world capturing impressions of human life and writing in the short story form.' Which leaves me, at least, concerned by this global village of short story writers apparently hell-bent on murder.

The collection opens with the most well-known writer in the assortment, Olive Senior, whose story 'Silent' – in which small children experience from under a bed the execution of their father ('he will watch, mesmerised, the blood pumping out of this father and creeping ever so slowly towards him') – is very good, but is too brutal as an opener and might have worked better if placed at a later point in the collection. Its bloody content jars with the chirpy close of the introduction: 'Enjoy!'

A few of the stories are genuinely brilliant. Drew Gummerson's 'Gus' reads like queer Vonnegut; with conspiracies, a time machine, the daring rescue of Iraqi scientists who are being held captive in Leicester Central Lending Library, and – of course – *The Sound of Music*. Nina Joshi-Ramsey's 'Through her Eyes' depicts a writer's visit to Benaras in carefully crafted and evocative prose; and Vivian Hassan-Lambert's story 'Konicek', describing a boat journey of a Jewish mother and daughters escaping Nazi-occupied Europe to New York, is a similarly compelling – yet understated – piece.

All in all, this is an uneven collection and, at times, is too random and too diverse. Some stories work well together; others less so. This is a book that rewards perseverance, and there are some beautiful moments, but the opening spate of blood might have deterred even the ghoulish Poe.

Abigail Ward, Nottingham Trent University

Notes on Contributors

Dinesh Allirajah, short story writer and jazz poet, was born in London to Sri Lankan parents, and is based in Liverpool. He co-founded Liverpool's Asian Voices, Asian Lives writers and performers' collective, and has performed and given workshops in European countries, Bangladesh, and Nigeria. His publications include the short story collection *A Manner Of Speaking* (2004); and individual pieces in anthologies such as *The Book Of Liverpool* and *ReBerth* (both 2008).

Moniza Alvi was born in Pakistan and grew up in Hertfordshire. She has published six collections of poetry of which the most recent are *Split World: Poems 1990-2005* (2008) and *Europa* (2008). She received a Cholmondeley Award in 2002. She lives in London and tutors for the Poetry School.

Muli Amaye went to Manchester Metropolitan University in 1998 to study English and discovered a love of writing that complemented her lifelong love of reading. An MA in Creative Writing followed. She is currently writing her PhD in Creative Writing at Lancaster University. Her writing and academic interests are centred around migration, memory, and notions of home.

Tanya Chan-Sam, a South African writer in Sheffield, has published in *180 Degrees* (2005), *Tell Tales 3* (2006), *Sable* (2006). *Mr Mohani* is her collection of short stories (2008). She has performed at Off the Shelf, Spit Lit, Sunday Salon (New York), Busboys and Poets (Washington) and GWU (Philadelphia).

Debjani Chatterjee's latest collection is *Words Spit and Splinter* (2009) and she recently edited *Raising their Voices: Poems by Children in Burngreave* (2008). She is a patron of Survivors' Poetry and a RLF Fellow (2006-2009). In 2008 she received an MBE for services to Literature and won First Prize in the Muse India Poetry Translation Competition.

Ian Duhig has published five books of poetry, most recently *The Speed of Dark* (2006) which was a Poetry Book Society Choice and was shortlisted for the T.S. Eliot and Costa Poetry Prizes. He has won a Forward Prize and the National Poetry Competition twice. He is presently working on a new book of poems, provisionally titled 'Jericho Shanty'.

Lucy Evans is completing a PhD in Caribbean literature at the University of Leeds. She has articles on Mark McWatt, Paul Gilroy and Dionne Brand forthcoming in the *Journal of Commonwealth Literature*, the *South Atlantic Quarterly* and the *Caribbean Quarterly*. She is co-editing a collection of critical essays on Caribbean short stories, to be published by Peepal Tree Press.

Fadia Faqir is a Jordanian/British writer based in Durham, UK. Her work has been translated into fifteen languages and published in eighteen countries. Her third novel *My Name is Salma* (US title *The Cry of the Dove*) was published in 2007. The prologue of her fourth and forthcoming novel, *At the Midnight Kitchen*, was published in Weber and won their fiction award 2009.

Corinne Fowler works on the AHRC *Moving Manchester* project for which she won Lancaster University's Best Researcher Faculty award. She is the author of several short stories and a critical study entitled *Chasing Tales: travel writing, journalism and the history of British ideas about Afghanistan* (2004). She has edited *From Fiji to the Cannibal Islands* (forthcoming, 2010) and co-edited *Migration Stories* (2009) and *Travel Writing and Ethics* (forthcoming 2010).

Danielle Fuller is Senior Lecturer and Director of the Regional Centre for Canadian Studies at Birmingham University. She has published articles about Canadian literary culture and *Writing the Everyday: Women's Textual Communities in Atlantic Canada* (2004), which was awarded the Gabrielle Roy Prize. She is collaborating with DeNel Rehberg Sedo on a monograph arising from an AHRC project investigating contemporary mass-mediated reading events in three nation states.

Sarah Gibson is Lecturer in the Department of English at the University of Surrey. She has co-edited *Mobilizing Hospitality: The Ethics of Social Relations in a Mobile World* (2007). Her articles have been published in several journals, including *Journal for Cultural Research*, *Third Text*, *Space and Culture*, and *Tourist Studies*.

Basir Sultan Kazmi has published collections of Urdu poetry – *Moj-e-Khayal* (1997), *Chaman Koi Bhi Ho* (2008) – as well as an Urdu play, *Bisaat* (1987), which was translated and published as *The Chess Board* (1997). His translations of ghazals, which include 'A Little Bridge' (1997) and 'Generations of Ghazals' (2003), have appeared in several magazines/anthologies. He is currently Royal Literary Fund Fellow at the University of Bradford.

Shamshad Khan's performances have included collaborations with musicians and beatboxers. Her work explores themes of power, loss, identity and love. She runs creative writing workshops for all age groups. Her solo poetry collection, *Megalomaniac*, was published in 2007.

Graham Mort lectures at Lancaster University and is a member of the Moving Manchester research project. He has worked extensively in Africa for the British Council in literature development. His latest book of poems, *Visibility*, was published in 2007; *Touch*, a collection of stories, will appear in 2010.

Kate Pahl is a Senior Lecturer in Education at the University of Sheffield. She is interested in community projects that focus on identities in postcolonial contexts. She has been involved in research funded by the Museums Libraries and Archives council on digital storytelling in families together with community literacy and art projects in Barnsley and Rotherham. She is the author of a forthcoming book on literacy, learning and artefacts to be published in 2010.

Andy Pollard is Senior Lecturer in Visual Culture and Management at Sheffield Hallam University. He manages a commercial gallery in Yorkshire and his research interests include museums and non-western culture.

James Procter is Reader in Modern English and Postcolonial Literature at Newcastle University. He is the editor of *Writing Black Britain* (2000), author of *Dwelling Places* (2003) and *Stuart Hall* (2004). He has also co-authored *Comparing Postcolonial Diasporas* (2008). He is currently involved in a three-year collaborative AHRC project examining the relationship between reading, location, and migration.

Artist **Zahir Rafiq** works with both traditional and new digital media on graphic design and website design. His work seeks to highlight the valuable contributions to British society made by Muslims from all walks of life. He was commissioned by South Yorkshire Police to produce artwork for a poster campaign and Eid card. He is involved in workshops for schools where pupils learn about the Islamic faith through art.

Renuka Rajaratnam is a researcher at the Manchester Metropolitan University Research Institute producing work on issues of diaspora, identity, and globalization. She has published since 2000 in the *Literary Review*, *The Hindu* (India), *The International Journal of Humanities*, and *The Journal of Contemporary South Asia*. Her work in progress is a book entitled *Imagined Diasporas of the Elsewhere in British-Asian cities*.

John Siddique is the author of *The Prize* (2005), *Poems from a Northern Soul* (2007), *Recital – An Almanac* (2009). He has edited *Transparency* (2006), and co-authored *Four Fathers* (2006). His children's book *Don't Wear it on Your Head* (2007) was shortlisted for the CLPE Poetry Award. He was this year's British Council Writer in Residence at Cal State Los Angeles.

John Whale is Professor of Romantic Literature in the School of English at the University of Leeds. He is the author of books on Thomas De Quincey, imagination, and John Keats. His current projects include studies of Romantic period pugilism and of William Roscoe's Liverpool. He is a co-editor of *Stand* magazine.

Volume 10 2010
Singapore
Focus on Michael Ondaatje

Forthcoming issues include:
Locating the Caribbean; (Con)figuring Sports
Postcolonial Europe

All titles subject to confirmation

Routledge
Taylor & Francis Group

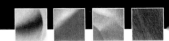

Journal of Postcolonial Writing

Affiliated to the Postcolonial Studies Association UK

EDITOR:
Janet Wilson, *University of Northampton, UK*

ASSOCIATE EDITORS:
Sarah Lawson Welsh, *York St. John University College, UK*
Fiona Tolan, *Liverpool John Moores University, UK*
Christina Sandru, *The University of Northampton, UK*

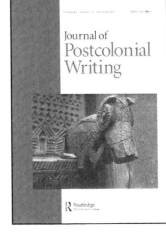

The *Journal of Postcolonial Writing* (previously *World Literature Written in English)* is an academic journal devoted to the study of literature written in English and published throughout the world. In particular it aims to explore the interface between the postcolonial writing of the modern global era and the economic forces of production which increasingly commodify culture.

This approach embraces the deterritorialised nationalisms, the new ethnicities which intersect with and cut across national boundaries, 'new margins' created by global economic practices, global technologies and commodities, and redefinitions of the local that globalisation catalyses. A particular focus is on the reshaping of inner maps of the metropolis through the ethnic, diasporic voices and the alternative and interstitial modes of writing associated with the new margins.

In addition *Journal of Postcolonial Writing* aims to publish:

- Interviews and profiles of postcolonial writers and theorists.
- Reviews of critical studies of contemporary writing.
- Selections of poetry and short prose fiction.

To sign up for tables of contents, new publications and citation alerting services visit **www.informaworld.com/alerting**

updates
Taylor & Francis Group

Register your email address at **www.tandf.co.uk/journals/eupdates.asp** to receive information on books, journals and other news within your areas of interest.

Powered by
informaworld

For further information, please contact Customer Services at either of the following:
T&F Informa UK Ltd, Sheepen Place, Colchester, Essex, CO3 3LP, UK
Tel: +44 (0) 20 7017 5544 Fax: 44 (0) 20 7017 5198
Email: subscriptions@tandf.co.uk Website: www.tandf.co.uk/journals

Taylor & Francis Inc, 325 Chestnut Street, Philadelphia, PA 19106, USA
Tel: +1 800 354 1420 (toll-free calls from within the US)
or +1 215 625 8900 (calls from overseas) Fax: +1 215 625 2940
Email: info@taylorandfrancis.com Website: www.taylorandfrancis.com
When ordering, please quote: XB90402A

View an online sample issue at
www.tandf.co.uk/journals/jpw